PLAYFUL HOODIES

PLAYFUL HOODIES

25 Reinvented Sweatshirts for Dress Up, for Costumes & for Fun

MARY RASCH

LARK

LARK

An Imprint of Sterling Publishing
387 Park Avenue South
New York, NY 10016

ISBN 978-1-4547-0800-1

Library of Congress Cataloging-in-Publication Data

Rasch, Mary.
 Playful hoodies : 25 reinvented sweatshirts for dress up, for costumes & for fun / Mary Rasch. -- 1st edition.
     pages cm
 Includes bibliographical references and index.
 ISBN 978-1-4547-0800-1 (alk. paper)
 1. Children's costumes. 2. Sewing. I. Title.
 TT560.R37 2014
 646.4'06--dc23
                    2013039055

Distributed in Canada by Sterling Publishing
c/o Canadian Manda Group, 165 Dufferin Street
Toronto, Ontario, Canada M6K 3H6
Distributed in the United Kingdom by GMC Distribution Services
Castle Place, 166 High Street, Lewes, East Sussex, England BN7 1XU
Distributed in Australia by Capricorn Link (Australia) Pty. Ltd.
P.O. Box 704, Windsor, NSW 2756, Australia

For information about custom editions, special sales, and premium and corporate purchases, please contact Sterling Special Sales at 800-805-5489 or specialsales@sterlingpublishing.com.

Email academic@larkbooks.com for information about desk and examination copies.
The complete policy can be found at larkcrafts.com.

Manufactured in China

2 4 6 8 10 9 7 5 3 1

larkcrafts.com

contents

Introduction

In an effort to make something special for a friend who was expecting her first baby, I decided I would make a costume for her little girl based on my friend's favorite animal. I sat down at my sewing machine, and a short while later, I had a unicorn costume made from only a hooded sweatshirt and fleece. At the time, I was at a crafting retreat with a room full of talented women who made me feel good as the "oohs" and "ahhs" filled the room. At that moment, the idea for *Playful Hoodies* was born.

You can find that first outfit, the Unicorn, on page 100. Turn to page 94 to find Little Red Riding Hood. Do you know a child who would like to be a prince, a princess, or a frog? How about a bunny, a fox, or a puppy? They're all here, and with just a few simple tools and some fleece, you can create personalized costumes for the little ones in your life.

As with my previous book, *Fleece Hat Friends*, I made the patterns easy to follow and the final products a hoot to wear. Comfort is a priority. If you are going play princess all day, your crown can't dig into your head, and it better not fall off. If you are saving the world in your superhero costume, you shouldn't constantly have to ask your mom to reattach your cape.

I hope you enjoy the projects in this book as much as I enjoyed creating them. Have fun making them, and savor the delight when sharing them with your child. Let the hours of entertainment begin!

Getting Started

Fun to make and comfortable to wear, these whimsical outfits made from simple hooded sweatshirts are a delight. This book takes you through easy-to-understand instructions to create 31 adorable projects. Their uses are endless in imaginative play, as Halloween costumes, or as part of your fashion bug's everyday garb. It's time to take that boring old sweatshirt and make it into a true favorite.

The History of the Hooded Sweatshirt

There's a reason why hooded sweatshirts are so popular. Yes, they are warm, comfortable, and durable. They also provide additional protection from the elements for our hands and head by having a muff sewn on the front and, of course, the iconic hood. Because of this accessory, these sweatshirts are often referred to as "hoodies." Like jeans, hoodies have become a mainstream fashion that has stood the test of time, exceeding their original purpose.

The first hooded sweatshirt was manufactured in the early 1930s in response to the needs of football and track athletes who waited in freezing temperatures on the sidelines, cold-storage warehouse workers, and tree surgeons in cold climates. Long underwear wasn't always practical, and a popular sporting goods company began producing double-thick shirts with hoods. The rest is history.

What Kind of Hooded Sweatshirt Should I Get?

There are basically two types of hooded sweatshirts: those with zippers and those without. On most projects in the book, either type is fine to use, but there are some that require one type or the other. See the "Before You Begin" section at the beginning of each project to find out which type is best to use.

In some stores, sweatshirts may be considered a seasonal item, so you might have an easier time stocking up on the colors you need in the fall. However, if you are having a hard time locating a few of the more unique colors, or if you are working on your sweatshirts in the summer, you can purchase them online or through promotional advertising companies.

You'll find out whether pants are an important accessory in the "Before You Begin" section of each project. Sometimes it's hard to find matching sweatpants, and if this is the case, you can purchase matching sweatpants and sweatshirts online.

The projects in this book were made with cotton/polyester blend sweatshirts, which are breathable, easy to wash, and generally easy to sew. However, feel free to take liberties with the style of hoodie, the colors, and the material of the sweatshirt for your project. Think outside the box when considering your options.

The Anatomy of a Sweatshirt

hoodie

zipper

sleeves

cuff

front pockets

lower hem

Sizes

All patterns in this book are made for sizes 2T through XL youth. Yes, that's right! You can make these outfits for almost any child in your life.

Keep in mind that these sizes are estimates only. You'll need to purchase the size that best fits your child and make any adjustments for templates and embellishments as noted in the projects.

Age	Size Chart
18 - 24 Months	2T
2-3 Years	3T
3-4 Years	4T/XS
4-6 Years	S
6-8 Years	M
8-10 Years	L
10 Years +	XL

Washing Instructions

Definitely machine-wash your sweatshirt before you begin a project because it may shrink a bit. Machine-washing will also remove its sizing, which is a treatment applied to the fabric to help it keep its shape and resist stains during shipment. However, once you are done with the project, I suggest hand-washing. There are so many embellishments that adorn these outfits, and you'll want to ensure the integrity of the stitching. If machine-washing them is a must (I would not suggest this for costumes such as the Gnome or Wizard), put the sweatshirt in a laundry bag to protect its embellishments. Set your washing machine to the delicate cycle with cold water. After washing is complete, lay your outfit flat to dry.

Materials

Fleece

Fleece is so easy to work with. That's why I have opted for most embellishments to be made from this non-raveling, forgiving, and easy-to-care for material. How else do I love fleece? Let me count the ways. I love the stretch, which aids in its forgiving nature. I love the bright array of colors offered. I love its warmth and softness and the fact that stitches sink into its fuzz. Where are the violins? Okay, I'll stop.

On an informational note, fleece comes in two different types: regular-grade fleece and anti-pill fleece. The anti-pill fleece has been treated, which gives it a textured look. Although both fleece types are fine to use, over time, the non-pill fleece will hold up better.

It's easier to tell the right and wrong side of anti-pill fleece. With regular-grade fleece, it can be hard to tell the difference, but the selvage edges will always turn up toward the right side of the fabric. What if you can't tell which side is the selvage edge? Grab your material and give it a stretch. The edge that does not stretch as easily is the selvage edge. Once you have figured this out, go ahead and mark the wrong side with a fabric pen/pencil or chalk.

As mentioned above, fleece comes in quite an array of colors. If you do not have a huge selection in your stash or at your local fabric store, feel free to select different colors than those that are used in the patterns. Customize these sweatshirts to show your style.

Thread

I suggest using a good-quality thread, such as 100 percent polyester. Although your fleece will hide most of your stitches, I recommend using a color to match the fleece you are sewing. White thread works well, too.

Polyester Fiberfill

This product is a great item for giving dimension to many of your sweatshirt embellishments. Get ready to stuff bee stingers, monster horns, frog eyes, and more.

You can use polyester fiberfill or a more environmentally-friendly product, which does the same thing as its polyester cousin but is instead made with 100 percent annually renewable resources.

Batting

The Shark's fin is the only project that requires batting; just a small amount of it will create a perfect, not-too-stuffed-look for your little Jaws.

Crocheted Headband Ribbon

Usually, you will see this type of elastic ribbon used for headbands, especially for babies. However, you will be adding another use to its repertoire by using it as a waistband in projects

such as the Fairy and the Princess. The holes in the crocheted material are perfect for looping tulle to create a skirt.

Glue

You will be using machine-washable fabric glue, industrial-strength glue, and hot glue throughout these projects. Any type of washable fabric glue will do. Be careful with the industrial-strength glue—you can glue your fingers together. Remember, hot glue is hot. Use caution.

Pipe Cleaners

These are a perfect way to add structure to certain embellishments. Purchase standard-size pipe cleaners. You can choose any color; they will be covered with fleece.

Craft Fur

Head to your local craft store to find sheets of 9 x 12-inch (23 x 33 cm) white craft fur for the Gnome's and Wizard's hair and beards. You may want to keep a lint roller handy when you cut into the material, because it will shed for a while. However, the final touch the fur gives the outfit is totally worth the shedding.

Interfacing

Look for interfacing that is thick and stiff. You can find it at your fabric store. It will be used to give the Wizard's and Gnome's hats their cone shape.

Ribbon and Trim

There are so many ribbons and trims to choose from. It's fine to use exactly what is shown in the book or to choose something a little different. You will use ruffle ribbon trim, tulle ruffle trim, organza ribbon, satin ribbon, and grosgrain ribbon. I found all of these sold by the roll, but you can purchase them by the yard, too.

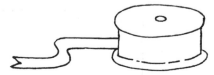

Felt

You'll be using three types of felt in these projects: craft felt, stiffened craft felt, and blended wool felt. All come in thin sheets of various sizes, but their characteristics are quite different. Craft felt is often used in kids' crafting projects and is made from non-woven fibers of polyester, rayon, acrylic, or viscose blends. Similar is the stiffened craft felt that is made from the same materials. The difference is that a stiffener is added to make the material rigid. Blended wool is, of course, made with real wool but also blended with rayon. The result is a more textured, yet soft, luxurious fabric. The blended wool felt may cost a bit more, but all three types of felt are reasonably priced.

Tulle

Yes, you can purchase tulle from the bolt, but for these projects, I recommend buying it by the roll. See the Tutu-torial on page 34 for a timesaving way to cut hundreds of strips for all of the tutus you see. The rolls will make the cutting simple.

As your outfit is worn over and over again, you may find that eventually the tulle strips bunch up. Don't worry—you can regain the flowing smooth strips of tulle once again. Lay your outfit on a flat surface. Gently sort through the strips from one side of the skirt to the other and pull the bunched strips straight. Hang the outfit upright and lightly spray the tulle with water from a spray bottle. Run your fingers through the strips and let them air-dry.

If you live in a dry climate where static electricity can ruin the flow of any good outfit, you may want to use a spray that eliminates the cling. You can find this spray at any discount store near the laundry supplies. Spray it onto the tulle and let it dry.

Elastic

I use 1-inch-wide (2.5 cm) elastic for the waistband of the tutus, because it can be sewn together to create a strong hold instead of tying thinner elastic together, where the knot could loosen over time.

Netting

Netting is an easy material to use to make the wings for the Bumblebee. It's similar to Tulle but has bigger holes and a bit more structure. Search for it in your fabric store, sold by the bolt.

Wooden Dowel

You can find these at craft or hardware stores. You will need dowels that are ¼ inch (6 mm) in diameter for the magic wands.

Buttons, Jewels, and Beads

Used as embellishments, the most common buttons you will need are black buttons to represent eyes. I look for buttons that have a loop on the back. Any size is fine, depending upon what you prefer.

I also use large buttons that are designed to look like jewels, which are perfect for the Princess crown. If your Prince doesn't mind a little sparkle, feel free to bedazzle his crown, too.

Finally, red buttons are used on the Gingerbread Person outfit. My one suggestion is to go big!

Pom-Poms

You'll need pom-poms with diameters of 1 and 2 inches (2.5 and 5.1 cm) to use as toppers for antennas and fingertips.

Hook-and-Loop Tape

Thank you, George de Mestral, for inventing this great tool. Without you, our Ducky Feet surely wouldn't be so quack-tastic. When selecting the type of hook-and-loop tape you want to work with, size is the only thing that is of concern—go for a width of ¾ inch (1.9 cm).

Silk Flower Bunch

When selecting a silk flower bunch, look for a medium-size flower that will be petite enough for your little Fairy to wear in her hair as a wreath and along her waistband. If you are making the outfit for a tiny Fairy, then go for an even smaller flower.

Once you have selected your flowers, it's a good idea to test their colorfastness by placing one flower in a glass of water. After an hour or two, does the water still look clear? If the water has taken on the color of the flower, then that flower will run on the Fairy outfit when it's time to wash it. If the water is still clear, you're good to go.

Floral Tape

You can find floral tape at any craft store, and if you haven't already used it, you'll find it's a fun product. Purchase a shade of green that matches the stems on your silk flower bunch. *A tip:* The more you rub it with your fingers, the more it adheres.

Rickrack

This is the perfect frosting for the Gingerbread Person. Look for white jumbo rickrack, which can be found at most craft stores or ordered online.

Snaps

Use sew-on snaps on the bearded Gnome and Wizard if you are working with a zippered sweatshirt. It doesn't matter what size or what material they are made of.

Hooks and Eyes

These notions come in handy when adding the final touches on Little Red Riding Hood's cape. These small metal pieces are placed in discrete locations, such as behind the cape's bow, and are easy to sew in place.

Webbing

Webbing is a tightly woven fabric that's often used for straps or upholstery. But it may be hard to know what I'm referring to based solely on its definition. The picture below shows webbing that is used for the dog collar on the Puppy costume. A picture is worth a thousand words! You can find webbing online or at craft stores.

Black Bead-Stringing Wire

Used for the Rabbit's whiskers, black bead-stringing wire can be found in the jewelry section of your local craft store. Buy wire that is 0.015 inch (0.38 mm) in diameter.

Tools

Sewing Machine

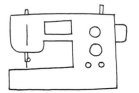

You may have a cranky old machine or one that happily hums along. Any sewing machine will get the job done. Making sure that your sewing machine is in proper working order will save your nerves. Go ahead and take this opportunity to get your machine tuned and grab a new, sharp needle, too. Note that the size of the needle depends on the thickness of your sweatshirt and fleece. Your local fabric store can help you determine what the best size is for the materials you have selected. Generally, a size 14 needle will work.

Sewing Needles

Standard needles will do the trick for the majority of the projects. However, in the Scarecrow instructions, you will find that a yarn needle, which has a point that can go through sweatshirt material, is needed.

Scissors, Rotary Cutters, Grids, and Mats

There is a large amount of cutting involved in these projects, and sometimes it is best to use scissors, while other times a rotary cutter is the way to roll ... with your grid and mat, of course.

The grid is a tool used to keep your cuts straight. Finger guards can be bought and attached to the grid. My experience? If you like the tips of your fingers, go ahead and get the guard.

A self-healing mat is a tool that will extend the life of your rotary cutter blade. It also keeps your work surface protected.

Pins

If you're like me, your crafting area can turn into a danger zone after a good sewing venture, due to misplaced pins. So, invest in pins that have colored bead heads. If they fall, you can find them. Problem solved.

Basic Sewing Tool Kit

Grid	Sewing Machine
Marking Tools	Sewing Needles
Mat	Tape Measure or Ruler
Pins	
Rotary Cutter	Thread
Scissors	

Tracing Paper, Tissue Paper, or Interfacing

To keep these sweet patterns safe for future use, keep them intact inside the book. Instead of cutting out the patterns, use tracing paper, light-colored tissue paper, or interfacing. Interfacing is a great material, because it doesn't slip when placed on fabric.

Note that some patterns in the back of the book will need to be enlarged, but this can easily be done with your own printer/scanner, or you can get assistance at your local copy/printing store.

Razor Saw

You will need to cut the wooden dowel. A razor saw is a smaller version of a handsaw and will cut the dowel neatly.

Lighter

To stop ribbon from fraying, find the lighter in the junk drawer and say goodbye to damaged ribbon ends. Just. Be. Careful.

Marking Tools

It's up to you which marking tools you would like to use; tailor's chalk, fabric markers and pens, pins, water-soluble pencils, or a tracing wheel with dressmaker's paper are all options. There is no one tool that will work on the variety of materials you will be working with, so decide which works best for you based on the color and type of fabric you have chosen.

Wire Cutters

Find the wire cutters in the toolbox, because you'll be snipping the wires in the floral bunches.

Fine-Grain Sandpaper

Sandpaper comes in an array of different "grits"—coarse, medium, fine, and very fine. Find a fine or very fine sandpaper, which is anywhere between 150 and 280 grit.

Craft Paint and Brush

You'll be painting the dowel used for the Magic Wand. Use paint that won't rub off when touched, such as craft paint. You'll also need a small brush such as an artist's paintbrush.

Rubber Gloves

Rubber gloves will save your fingertips when you're pulling yarn through sweatshirt material, which can be very resistant!

Adding Capes

You'll be hand-sewing a cape to the sweatshirt for the Wizard, Prince, Princess, Knight, and Superhero costumes. These figures show you the placement and folding pattern you'll need to follow in order to give maximum flow factor to your little caped wonder!

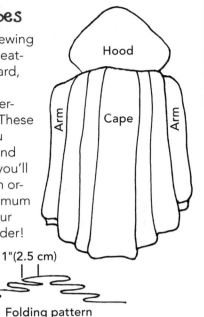

1"(2.5 cm)

Folding pattern

A Note About Seams and Stitching

Most seams are ¼ inch (6mm) throughout the book unless otherwise noted. Before you begin your project, double-check where the ¼-inch (6mm) mark is on your sewing machine. It will make a difference in the outcome of your project if you sway from this seam allowance.

You'll see that the individual project templates are marked with lines where I recommend machine-stitching and hand-stitching the pieces. All topstitching is ⅜ inch (1.0 cm). Note that for most attachments (ears, horns, spots, eyes), you can use whatever stitch you like. I tend to go with a ladder stitch—if the stitch shows, it will look nice.

Pirouette!

Roar!

Command a Kingdom!

the projects

Whether your little one is looking for the perfect Halloween costume or simply wants an imaginative outfit to wear to school, you're sure to find something in these pages that will provide hours of playtime fun.

So pick up your needle and thread, grab some fleece, turn the page, and get ready to embark on a playful adventure!

Cast a spell!

Save the world!

Gnome

Gnome

tools & materials

Basic Sewing Tool Kit (page 14)

Gnome/Wizard Template
   (page 112)

Dark green hooded sweatshirt

3 sheets of white craft fur
   (4 sheets may be necessary
   for larger sizes), 9 x 12 inches
   (22.9 x 30.5 cm) each

2 sew-on snaps (if using a
   zippered hoodie)

½ yard (45.7 cm) of rigid
   interfacing

36 inches square (91.4 cm) of red
   wool felt

Before You Begin

When selecting your hoodie, you can choose one that has a zipper down the front or you can choose one without. The instructions are written for both types, but it is easier if you have a sweatshirt without a zipper. Coordinating sweatpants are nice but not necessary to complete the outfit.

Instructions

1 Lay one sheet of the craft fur, with the wrong side facing up, on a flat surface and lay the sweatshirt hood on top of it. Cut the craft fur to follow the curved edge of the back of the hood, adding about ½ inch (1.3 cm) to the curved edge for wrapping purposes. Sew the straight edge of the craft fur to the front edge of the hood. Sew the top edge of the craft fur along the centerline of the hood all the way down to the back of the neck (figure 1). Repeat this step with a second sheet of craft fur for the other side of the hood. For larger sizes, you may need to add sections of a third sheet of craft fur to cover the entire hood.

cut

craft
fur

hood

figure 1

2 Create the beard from the last piece of craft fur. On one short edge, fold two corners up so that the wrong sides face each other. Then fold the edges of the beard in one more time to create a narrow point. Hand-sew the folded edges down. Cut a triangular section out of the top of the craft fur to fit the open section of the hood (figure 2).

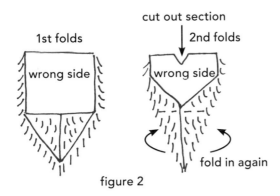

1st folds
cut out section
2nd folds
wrong side
wrong side
fold in again

figure 2

3 If you have a sweatshirt without a zipper, tuck the top edge of the beard into the craft fur or "hair" of the gnome and hand-sew it in place along the top edge. Separate craft fur pieces blend nicely together if you tuck the rough edge into the fur of the other piece. Let the rest of the beard hang, unsewn.

If you have a sweatshirt with a zipper, sew snaps to the top corners of the beard. Place the other side of the snap beneath the existing hair (figure 3). The wearer can unsnap the beard if he or she wants to unzip the sweatshirt.

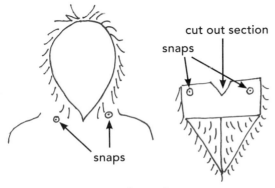

snaps
cut out section
snaps
snaps

figure 3

4 Cut one Hat piece from the rigid interfacing using the Gnome/Wizard template. Fold the interfacing into a cone, overlapping the straight edges, and hot glue these edges together. Make sure the glue is completely set before going to the next step.

5 Cut one Hat piece from the red wool felt using the template. Fold the hat so that the right sides are facing in and machine-sew along the straight edge as marked on the template. Turn the hat right side out and nest the interfacing cone inside the felt hat. Tuck and pin the red felt over the bottom edge of the cone and machine-sew it to secure the fabric.

6 Attach the hat to the top of the hood by tacking it in place multiple times.

Wizard

tools & materials

Basic Sewing Tool Kit (page 14)
Gnome/Wizard Template (page 112)
Wizard Templates (page 123)
Beard Figures (pages 18-19)
Adding Capes Figures (page 15)
Black hooded sweatshirt
Royal blue fleece:
    1 yard (91.4 cm) for sizes 2T–3T
    1¼ yards (114.3 cm) for size 4T/XS
    1½ yards (137 cm) for sizes S–M
    1¾ yards for sizes L–XL
¼ yard (22.9 cm) of gold fleece
3 sheets of white craft fur
    (4 sheets may be necessary for
    larger sizes), 9 x 12 inches
    (22.9 x 30.5 cm) each
2 sew-on snaps (for zippered
    hoodies)
Washable fabric glue
½ yard (45.7 cm) of rigid interfacing

Before You Begin

When selecting your hoodie, you can choose one that has a zipper down the front or you can choose one without. The instructions are written for both types, but it is easier if you have a sweatshirt without a zipper. Matching sweatpants are nice but not necessary to complete the outfit.

Note that you'll be referring to the same figures used for the Gnome's beard to make the Wizard's beard.

Instructions

1 Lay one sheet of the craft fur, with the wrong side facing up, on a flat surface and place the sweatshirt hood on top of it. Cut the craft fur to follow the curved edge of the back of the hood, adding about ½ inch (1.3 cm) to the curved edge for wrapping purposes. Sew the straight edge of the craft fur to the front edge of the hood. Sew the top edge of the craft fur along the center line of the hood all the way down to the back of the neck (see figure 1, page 18). Repeat this step with a second sheet of craft fur for the other side of the hood. For larger sizes, you may need to add sections of a third sheet of craft fur to cover the entire hood.

2 Create the beard from the last piece of craft fur. On one short edge, fold two corners up so that the wrong sides face each other. Then fold the edges of the beard in one more time to create a narrow point. Hand-sew the folded edges down. Cut a triangular section out of the top of the craft fur to fit the open section of the hood (see figure 2, page 19).

3 If you have a sweatshirt without a zipper, tuck the top edge of the beard into the craft fur or "hair" of the wizard and hand-sew it in place along the top edge. Separate craft-fur pieces blend nicely together if you layer them correctly. Let the rest of the beard hang, unsewn.

If you have a sweatshirt with a zipper, sew snaps to the top corners of the beard. Place the other side of the snap beneath the existing hair (figure 3, page 19). The wearer can unsnap the beard when he or she wants to unzip the sweatshirt.

4 For the cape, cut the blue fleece to the following measurement, depending on what size sweatshirt you have (you'll be using the remaining ½ yard [45.7 cm] of fleece for the Hat):

Sweatshirt Size	Fleece for the Cape
2T–3T	½ yard square (45.7 cm)
4T/XS	¾ yard square (68. 6 cm)
S–M	1 yard square (91.4 cm)
L–XL	1¼ yards square (114.3 cm)

5 You will be hand-sewing the cape onto the sweatshirt, so grab your needle and thread. Fold the cape in half to find the middle. At this center point, begin pinning the cape to the middle of the back neck of the sweatshirt, under the hood. You will be folding the material under in 1-inch (2.5 cm) folds to give the cape some fullness (see Adding Capes figures, page 15). I ended my material before it reached the front of the costume so it is always parted a bit. It really doesn't matter how you sew on the cape as long as it looks uniform on both sides and stays on for the long haul.

6 Cut five Star pieces and three Moon pieces from gold fleece using the Wizard templates. Stagger the Stars and Moons around the robe and glue them in place using washable fabric glue. Once the glue dries, you can hand- or machine-sew the edges down.

7 Cut one Hat piece from the rigid interfacing using the Gnome/Wizard template. Fold the interfacing into a cone, overlapping the straight edges, and hot glue these edges together. Make sure the glue is completely set before going on to the next step.

8 Cut one Hat piece from the royal blue fleece using the template. Fold the hat so that the right sides are facing in and sew along the straight edge as marked on the template. Turn the hat right side out and nest the interfacing cone inside the fleece hat. Tuck and pin the fleece over the bottom edge of the cone and machine-sew it to secure the fabric.

9 Cut three more Star pieces from gold fleece using the template. Stagger the Stars around the hat and glue them in place using washable fabric glue. Once the glue is dried, you can hand-sew the edges down. **Note:** You don't have to insert your needle all the way through the interfacing layer when hand-sewing.

10 Attach the hat to the top of the hood by tacking it in place in multiple spots.

See the instructions for the Wizard's Magic Wand on the following page to whip up a magical accessory!

Wizard's Magic Wand

tools & materials

Basic Sewing Tool Kit (page 14)

Magic Wand Template (page 115)

Fine-grain sandpaper

18-inch (45.7 cm) length of wooden
 dowel, ¼ inch (6 mm) in diameter

Black craft paint

Artist's paintbrush

1 sheet of yellow stiffened craft felt,
 12 x 18 inches (30.5 x 45.7 cm)

Hot glue gun and glue sticks

When I was preschooler, I had a magic wand, and with tireless desperation I twirled, and whirled, and shook that wand with every ounce of pixie dust in me trying to turn my older sister into a pumpkin. May this new and improved version bring you nothing but magical moments.

Instructions

1 Sand down any rough spots on the dowel until it is smooth for little hands. Paint the dowel with the black craft paint and set it aside to dry.

2 Using the Magic Wand template, cut two Star pieces from the yellow stiffened craft felt, one with the template facing up and one with the template facing down. With wrong sides together, machine-sew a ⅛-inch (3 mm) seam around the edge of the star, leaving a ¼-inch (6 mm) opening at the base of the star as shown on the template. Trim all excess thread.

3 Place a dab of hot glue on one end of the dowel and carefully slide it into the opening at the base of the star. Allow time for the glue to dry before you let the magic begin.

Fairy

tools & materials

Basic Sewing Tool Kit (page 14)

Fairy Templates (page 111)

Light green hooded sweatshirt

2 yards (1.8 m) of light green crocheted headband ribbon

1 to 2 rolls of sparkle white tulle (see A Note About Tulle, right)

1 to 2 rolls of light pink tulle

1 to 2 rolls of light green tulle

Large piece of cardboard

4 sheets of white stiffened craft felt, each 12 x 18 inches (30.5 x 45.7 cm)

Washable fabric glue

3 silk flowers, one slightly larger than other two (you can use extras from the Floral Head Wreath, page 29)

A Note About Tulle

Tulle often comes in 25-yard (22.9m) rolls. Depending on the size of your skirt and the desired fullness, you'll need to purchase 25 to 50 yards (22.9 to 45.7m) of sparkle white, light pink, and light green tulle for your Fairy costume.

Before You Begin

When selecting your hoodie, pick one without a zipper in front; there are embellishments sewn onto the sweatshirt that would interfere with a zipper. Leggings are recommended to complete this outfit.

Instructions

1 Have your future fairy try on the sweatshirt so you can mark under the bust, because you'll be creating an empire waistline. Cut off the sweatshirt 1 inch (2.5 cm) below the markings.

2 Pin the roll of crocheted headband ribbon around the waist of the sweatshirt, starting and ending at the center back. Make sure you provide enough overlap for the crocheted ribbon to look continuous; trim off any excess.

Make sure that the bottom row of holes is hanging below the sweatshirt material so the tulle can be looped through it. Machine-sew the ribbon through its middle onto the sweatshirt.

3 Decide what length you would like the skirt to be: knee length, mid-calf, tea length, or ankle length. Once again, have your fairy try on the sweatshirt and measure from the bottom of the attached waistband to the desired length.

4 The easiest way to cut uniform pieces of tulle from a roll is to wrap the tulle around a piece of cardboard that is cut to the desired skirt length. When all of the tulle is wrapped, make one cut anywhere across the wrapping. You now have tulle double the desired skirt length, which is perfect because it will be folded in half. Cut one roll at a time in sparkle white, light pink, and light green; don't cut more from the second roll until you know you need it. (For more information on cutting tulle for a tutu, see the Tutu-torial on page 34.)

5 Decide on the color pattern you want for your skirt and lay out your strips of tulle accordingly. Fold a strip of tulle in half, creating a loop. At the center back of the sweatshirt, insert the loop through a hole from the back of the crocheted waistband to the front. Bring the ends of the tulle up through the loop and gently pull them to create a knot (figure 1). Repeat this knotting around the entire waistband, creating a skirt using all three colors.

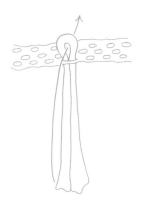

figure 1

6 Using the Fairy template, cut four Top Fairy Wing pieces from the stiffened craft felt, two with the pattern facing up and two with the pattern facing down. Match two of the Top Fairy Wings with wrong sides together and topstitch around the wing, ½ inch (1.3 cm) from the outer edge as shown on the template. Repeat for the other top fairy wing.

7 Using the template, cut four Bottom Fairy Wing pieces from the stiffened craft felt, two with the pattern facing up and two with the pattern facing down. Match two of the Bottom Fairy Wings with wrong sides together and topstitch around the wing, ½ inch (1.3 cm) from the outer edge as shown on the template. Repeat for the other bottom fairy wing.

8 Pin the bottom fairy wings onto the back of the sweatshirt on either side of the center, just above the waistband. Stitch over the topstitching as marked on the template to make the attachment marks less noticeable. Overlap the bottom fairy wings with the top fairy wings by about 3 inches (7.6 cm) and stitch over the topstitching to make the attachment marks less noticeable. You may need to tack down the wings in additional spots to keep them in place.

9 Glue three flowers on the front of the waistband, starting with the largest in the center and working your way out with the smaller two.

The Floral Head Wreath on page 29 and the Fairy's Magic Wand on page 30 will make your Fairy's costume complete!

Floral Head Wreath

tools & materials

Wire cutters

Bunch of silk flowers

Floral tape

Hot glue gun and glue sticks

Fabric scissors

8 feet (2.4 m) of light pink organza ribbon, ⅝ inch (1.6 cm) wide

8 feet (2.4 m) of white organza ribbon, ⅝ inch (1.6 cm) wide

Lighter

Before You Begin

This is a perfect accessory for the Fairy costume (page 24). Using the same flowers will tie the two together.

Instructions

1 Using wire cutters, snip each flower with its leaves from the bunch, leaving as much stem as possible. Carefully bend a slight curve into each stem.

2 Stagger the ends of two stems so there is a 2- to 3-inch (5.1 to 7.6 cm) section of the stem that is not overlapping. In two or three different locations, secure the stems together using floral tape. Continue to build up one side of the head wreath in this way, then start again from the other side until the wreath is approximately 20 to 22 inches (50.8 to 55.9 cm) in length. (Check for the correct size on your child's head.) Connect the two loose ends by overlapping them and securing them with floral tape.

Note: If the wreath is too full, feel free to pull off a few flowers and/or leaves.

3 To make the head wreath more durable, pluck off each flower one by one and hot-glue it back on. If the leaves run the risk of falling off, do the same for them.

4 Cut two pieces from the light pink organza ribbon and two pieces from the white organza ribbon, all at varying lengths; the example shown has ribbons cut 20 to 32 inches (50.8 to 81.3 cm) long. Tie each ribbon in half onto the back of the wreath and let the ends fall.

5 To prevent the organza ribbon from fraying, carefully wave the flame from a lighter near each end until it melts slightly.

Fairy's Magic Wand

tools & materials

Basic Sewing Tool Kit (page 14)

Magic Wand Template (page 115)

Hot glue gun and glue sticks

18-inch (45.7 cm) length of wooden dowel, ¼ inch (6 mm) in diameter

1 yard (91.4 cm) of light pink satin ribbon, ⅝ inch (1.6 cm) wide

5 yards (4.6 m) of light pink organza ribbon, ⅝ inch (1.6 cm) wide (optional)

5 yards (4.6 m) of white organza ribbon, ⅝ inch (1.6 m) wide (optional)

Lighter

1 sheet of white stiffened craft felt, 12 x 18 inches (30.5 x 45.7 cm)

Instructions

1 Place a dab of hot glue on one end of the dowel and place one end of the satin ribbon across the glue with about a ¼-inch (6 mm) overhang. Begin wrapping the ribbon at an angle toward the other end of the dowel, tucking the excess ribbon under the first wrap. Continue wrapping until you run out of ribbon. Glue the other end of the ribbon to the side of the dowel to ensure the ribbon doesn't unwind. Some of the dowel will be unwrapped, but it will be covered later by the star.

2 If you are making this wand for the Fairy costume (page 24), you may want to cut varying lengths of the organza ribbon, two pink and two white pieces. Tie them tightly around the dowel where the wrapped satin ribbon ends. Let the ends hang loose.

3 To prevent the organza ribbon from fraying, carefully wave a flame from a lighter near each end until they melt slightly.

4 Using the Magic Wand template, cut two Star pieces from the white stiffened craft felt, one with the template facing up and one with the template facing down. With wrong sides together, machine-sew a ⅛-inch (3 mm) seam around the edge of the star, leaving a ¼-inch (6 mm) opening at the base of the star as shown on the template. Trim all excess thread.

5 Place hot glue on the end of the dowel that hasn't been wrapped and carefully slide it into the opening at the base of the star. Allow time for the glue to dry before you let the magic begin.

Bumblebee

Bumblebee

tools & materials

Basic Sewing Tool Kit (page 14)
Bumblebee Template (page 107)
Black hooded sweatshirt
⅛ yard (11.4 cm) of black fleece
Decorative yellow ruffled ribbon or tulle:
12 feet (3.7 m) for sizes 2T–4T/XS
14 feet (4.3 m) for sizes S–M
16 feet (4.9 m) for sizes L–XL
2 large black pom-poms
Polyester fiberfill
⅔ yard (61 cm) of white netting

Before You Begin

When selecting your hoodie, it doesn't matter whether you pick one that has a zipper down the front or not. A zipper will not interfere with the embellishments. Refer to the Tutu-torial (page 34) to create a complementary black and yellow tutu, which adds some buzz to this sweet sweatshirt.

Instructions

1 Pin the decorative yellow ribbon or tulle around the waist along the waistband seam. Do the same for each wrist. Machine-sew the top edge of the ribbon in place.

2 Pin another row of decorative yellow ribbon or tulle above the previously sewn row, but make sure it is low enough on the waist so that it doesn't interfere with the openings of the sweatshirt pocket. Repeat for the wrists, placing the second row the same distance apart as the tulle around the waist. Machine-sew the ribbon in place.

3 To create the antennas, cut two 3 x 6-inch (7.6 x 15.2 cm) rectangles from black fleece. Starting at one short end, tightly roll one up like a sleeping bag and stitch along the long edge to keep the fleece from unrolling. Hand-sew a large pom-pom to one end and sew the other end to the top of the hood about 1 to 2 inches (2.5 to 5.1 cm) from the center seam. Repeat the rolling and sewing instructions to create and attach the second antenna.

4 Cut one Stinger piece from black fleece using the Bumblebee template. (**Note:** You are folding the fleece and placing the template on the fold.) Fold the stinger in half along the fold line with right sides together. Sew along the edge as marked on the template. Cut the excess material off the point of the stinger. Turn the material right side out and loosely fill the stinger with polyester fiberfill. Hand-sew the stinger to the back of the sweatshirt, being sure to place it high enough so that it doesn't interfere when the wearer sits down.

5 Cut a rectangle from the white netting using the measurements below. Gather the center of the netting to cinch up its length. Knot the center with thread to keep the wing formation in place. Attach the wings to the center of the back and tack each side to keep the wings upright.

Size	Netting Measurement
2T–4T/XS	12 x 20 inches (30.5 x 50.8 cm)
S–M	15 x 26 inches (38.1 x 66 cm)
L–XL	20 x 32 inches (50.8 x 81.3 cm)

This is one of the most di-sting-uishing projects of all. Your little honey will be the sweetest drone on the hive!

tutu-torial

tools & materials

Basic Sewing Tool Kit (page 14)

1-inch-wide (2.5 cm) elastic (length needed depends on waist measurement)

Large piece of cardboard

12-yard (11 m) rolls of 100 percent polyester tulle in desired colors (see chart below for quantities)

Before You Begin

Tulle often comes in 25-yard (22.9m) rolls. Determining how much tulle you need is the most difficult part of this project. It all depends on how full you like your tutu and the length you want. When the Tutu is paired with the Ladybug (page 50) or the Bumblebee (page 31) sweatshirts, I like to make it knee length and very full, so I buy a lot of tulle and make the knots quite close together. Use the table below only as a guide for knee-length Tutus, and make notes of your own measurements and preferences as you make yours.

Instructions

1 Measure the waist of your child. Make sure that she is relaxed, standing up straight, and not wearing bulky clothing. Add 2 inches (5.1 cm) to the waist measurement and cut the elastic to this length.

2 Overlap the ends of the elastic by 1 inch (2.5 cm) and sew a 1 x 1-inch (2.5 x 2.5 cm) square with an "X" sewn through it to secure the ends together.

3 Measure the length of the child from the waist to the knee. Add ½ inch (1.3 cm) to this measurement. Cut a piece of cardboard at least 6 inches (15.2 cm) wide to this length.

4 Beginning with one color, wrap a whole roll of tulle around the piece of cardboard. Once the tulle runs out, cut through the layers of tulle, creating strips that are double the desired length. Repeat this step with the other color(s).

5 Begin by tying the strips to the elastic. Fold a strip in half and bring it under the elastic waistband, forming a loop. Bring the ends of the strip up through the loop and pull them to form a knot (see figure 1). Keep the knot loose enough so that the elastic doesn't fold over. Continue tying these knots quite close to each other, and after about 15 strips, switch to the next color. Continue this pattern until the elastic band is completely covered and full. You can also create the Tutu from all one color.

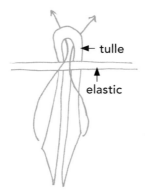

figure 1

Age	Waist Measurement	Knee Length	Rolls of Tulle Needed
1-2	15–18 inches (38.1–45.7 cm)	7–8 inches (17.8–20.3 cm)	2-3
2-3	18–20 inches (45.7–50.8 cm)	8–9 inches (20.3–22.9 cm)	3-4
3-4	20–22 inches (50.8–55.9 cm)	9–10 inches (22.9–25.4 cm)	4-5
5-6	21–23 inches (53.3–58.4 cm)	10–13 inches (25.4–33 cm)	5-6
6-7	22–24 inches (55.9–61 cm)	13–16 inches (33–40.6 cm)	6-8
8-10	24–26 inches (61–66 cm)	15–17 inches (38.1–43.2 cm)	8-9
10-11	25–27 inches (63.5–68.6 cm)	16–18 inches (40.6–45.7 cm)	9-10
12	27–28 inches (68.6–71.1 cm)	18–20 inches (45.7–50.8 cm)	10-11

Puppy

Puppy

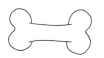

tools & materials

Basic Sewing Tool Kit (page 14)

Puppy Templates (page 118)

Gray hooded sweatshirt

¼ yard (22.9 cm) of black fleece

⅔ yard (61 cm) of 1 inch (2.5 cm) red webbing

1 sheet of gold stiffened craft felt, 12 x 18 inches (30.5 x 45.7 cm)

Industrial-strength glue

2 black buttons

Before You Begin

When selecting your hoodie, search for one that has a zipper down the front; this is where you'll attach the dog tag. Matching sweatpants are nice but not necessary to complete the outfit.

Instructions

1 Cut four Ear pieces from black fleece using the Puppy template. Match two ears right sides together. Sew along the curved edge, leaving the straight edge open as marked on the template. Turn the ear right side out and topstitch along the curved edge just sewn. Repeat these sewing instructions to create a second ear.

2 To give the ears more dimension, fold the outer edges near the straight end of the ear in toward the middle. Hand-sew the now-folded edges in place. Pin and sew the straight edges of the ears 2 to 3 inches (5.1 to 7.6 cm) apart on top of the hood. (See photo at left for reference.)

3 To create the collar, pin the red webbing around the neck along the seam that connects the hood to the sweatshirt. Wrap about 1 inch (2.5 cm) of the ends around the front edge of the hood to the inside, trim, and pin them in place. Machine-sew through the center of the webbing to secure it to the sweatshirt.

4 Cut two Dog Tag pieces from stiffened gold craft felt using the template. With wrong sides together, sew a ⅛-inch (3 mm) seam around the edge of the bone to connect the two felt pieces. Glue the bone onto the top of the zipper pull.

5 Depending on whether or not you have pants for your outfit and how spotted you would like your puppy to be, cut the desired number of spots from the black fleece using the Spot template. Place the spots where desired and hand-sew around the edge of each one.

6 To make the nose, use the Spot template and cut one more from black fleece. Fold it over the front edge on the top of the hood. Hand-sew around the edge of the nose on the top of the hood and the underside to secure it in place.

7 Hand-sew two black buttons centered above the nose for the eyes.

8 Cut two Tail pieces from black fleece using the template. With wrong sides together, sew around the curved edge, leaving the straight edge open. Turn the tail right side out. Center it on the back of the sweatshirt and hand-sew along the straight edge, securing it in place.

Owl

tools & materials

Basic Sewing Tool Kit (page 14)
Owl Templates (page 117)
Aqua hooded sweatshirt
½ yard (45.7 cm) of yellow fleece
Scrap of orange fleece
Scrap of white fleece
½ yard (45.7 cm) of brown fleece

Before You Begin

When selecting your hoodie, it doesn't matter whether you pick one that has a zipper down the front or not. The embellishments will not interfere with a zipper. Matching sweatpants are nice but not necessary to complete the outfit.

Instructions

1 Cut the Face piece from yellow fleece using the Owl template. Hand-sew it to the top of the hood just off the front edge.

2 Cut two Beak pieces from orange fleece using the template. Match the two pieces with right sides together and sew along the bottom two edges as marked on the template, leaving the top edges open. Turn the beak right side out and attach it to the owl Face piece, hand-sewing along the top two edges and overlapping the front edge of the hood.

3 Cut two Outer Eye pieces from white fleece using the template. Hand-sew the outer eyes to the Face piece, overlapping the beak as shown below.

4 Cut two Inner Eye pieces from brown fleece using the template. Hand-sew the inner eyes in the center of the Outer Eyes.

5 Cut two Ear pieces from orange fleece using the template. Fold in the two bottom corners of one triangle so the right side is facing out. Hand-sew the bottom edges together and hand-sew the ear directly above the Face piece where desired. Repeat the sewing instructions in this step to create and attach the second ear.

6 Cut many, many, many Feather pieces out of brown and yellow fleece using the template. How many should you cut? It all depends on how you prefer to space the feathers and the size of the sweatshirt. On the 2T costume shown, there are approximately 30 yellow feathers and 50 brown feathers. Start at the bottom of the sleeve and hand-sew the top of each feather to the sleeve, overlapping them. Continue to cut and sew feathers until you fill up the sleeves as desired.

Monster

Monster

tools & materials

Basic Sewing Tool Kit (page 14)
Monster Templates (page 116)
Aqua hooded sweatshirt
¼ yard (22.9 cm) of orange fleece
¼ yard (22.9 cm) of dark green fleece
1/8 yard (11.4 cm) of white fleece
Polyester fiberfill
2 black beads, 6 or 8 mm in diameter

Before You Begin

When selecting your hoodie, it doesn't matter whether you pick one that has a zipper down the front or not. The embellishments will not interfere with a zipper. Matching sweatpants are nice but not necessary to complete the outfit.

Instructions

1 Cut two 6½ x 8-inch (16.5 x 20.3 cm) rectangles from the orange fleece. With each rectangle, cut fringe 1 inch (2.5 cm) wide along each 8-inch (20.3 cm) side of the rectangle, leaving the center ½ inch (1.3 cm) of each rectangle uncut. (The uncut center is a sewing line.)

2 Cut four 6½ x 7-inch (16.5 x 17.8 cm) rectangles from the orange fleece. Just as you did in the previous step, cut fringe 1 inch (2.5 cm) wide along each 7-inch (17.8 cm) side of the rectangle, leaving the center ½ inch (1.3 cm) of each rectangle uncut. (The uncut center is a sewing line.)

3 Stack the two large rectangles on top of each other. At the very top of the hood, line up the short ends of the rectangles with the hood's front edge. Machine-sew down the ½-inch (1.3 cm) center of the rectangles along the centerline of the hood. To add some pizzazz to the hair, take two fringe pieces and loosely knot them together. Continue this throughout the hair. Repeat these sewing instructions for the smaller rectangles, only this time place one on either side of the large rectangles.

4 Using the Monster template, cut four Horn pieces from dark green fleece, two with the pattern facing up and two with the pattern facing down. Match up two Horn pieces with right sides together and machine-sew along the two curved edges, leaving the straight edge open. Turn the horn right side out and loosely stuff it with fiberfill. Repeat the sewing instructions in this step to create the second horn. Hand-sew the horns to either side of the hood nestled just below the hair.

5 Cut two Eye pieces out of white fleece using the template. Loosely baste around the outer edge of this circle and pull the thread to create a pouch. Stuff a small amount of fiberfill in the pouch, cinch it shut, and stitch the opening closed. Place a black bead on the center of the eye. Pass the needle and thread from the back of the eyeball to the front and thread the bead through its center hole. Repeat until the bead is secure. Pass back through the eyeball and pull the thread tight so that the bead sinks slightly into the eye. Repeat for the second eye. Hand-sew the eyes into the hair at the front of the hood.

6 Cut three Big Spot pieces and five Little Spot pieces out of dark green fleece using the template. Hand-sew the spots in small groupings on the front and back of the sweatshirt.

7 Cut four Hand pieces out of dark green fleece using the template. With right sides together, machine-sew along all edges marked on the template, leaving the long straight edge open. Turn the hand right side out and topstitch along the edges just sewn. Repeat the sewing instructions in this step to create the second hand. Turn the cuff of each sweatshirt sleeve inside out, and pin and hand-sew the straight edge of the hand to the cuff seam. Make sure the fleece hands line up with the top of the wearer's hands once the sweatshirt is on.

8 Cut two Teeth pieces out of white fleece using the template. With right sides together, machine-sew along the angled edges as marked on the template, leaving the long straight edge open. Flip the teeth right side out and topstitch along the edges just sewn. Center the teeth and hand-sew the straight edge to the inside of the hood about 1 inch (2.5 cm) from the front or along the seam line.

Rabbit

tools & materials

Basic Sewing Tool Kit (page 14)

Rabbit Templates (page 119)

White hooded sweatshirt

¼ yard (22.9 cm) of white fleece

¼ yard (22.9 cm) of pink fleece

Polyester fiberfill

36 inches (91.4 cm) of black bead-stringing wire, 0.015 inch (0.38 mm) in diameter

2 black beads, 6 or 8 mm in diameter

Before You Begin

When selecting your hoodie, it doesn't matter whether you pick one that has a zipper down the front or not. The embellishments will not interfere with a zipper. Matching sweatpants are nice but not necessary to complete the outfit.

Instructions

1 Cut two Ear pieces from white fleece and two Ear pieces from pink fleece using the Rabbit template. Make sure that you cut one of each color with the pattern facing up and one of each color with the pattern facing down. Match up a pink ear with a white ear, right sides together. Sew around the two curved edges, leaving the straight edge open as shown on the template. Turn the ear right side out and topstitch along the two edges just sewn. Repeat this step for the other ear. Pin and sew the straight edges of the ears 2 to 3 inches (5.1 to 7.6 cm) apart on the top of the hood.

2 Cut one Nose piece from pink fleece using the template. Baste around the outer edge and pull the thread to create a pouch. Stuff a small amount of fiberfill in this pouch, cinch it shut, and sew the opening closed. To create a nostril, bring your needle up from the back of the nose through one of the spots marked on your pattern. Loop your needle around the edge and back up through the same spot. Keep looping and pulling the thread tight. Repeat this step for the other nostril. Center the nose on the top of the hood about 1 inch (2.5 cm) from the front edge and hand-sew it on.

3 Cut three 12-inch (30.5 cm) strands of bead-stringing wire. Wrap one strand around the base of the nose and knot it so there are two equal lengths on each side. Repeat this two more times so there are six whiskers sprouting from the nose. Arrange the whiskers as desired.

4 Hand-sew two black beads just above the nose for the eyes.

5 Cut one Tail piece out of white fleece using the template. With scissors or a rotary cutter, grid, and mat, cut along the markings on the template, leaving the ½-inch (1.3 cm) section in the middle uncut. Starting at one short side, roll the strip like a sleeping bag and secure it by sewing through the center of the roll. Tightly wrap thread around the roll three times and bring the needle through the center once again. Secure the pom-pom you just made with a knot and sew it to the back of the sweatshirt high enough so the tail is not in the way when your rabbit sits down. Fluff the tail and trim any pieces as necessary.

Bear

Bear

tools & materials

Basic Sewing Tool Kit (page 14)
Bear Templates (page 106)
Dark brown hooded sweatshirt
⅛ yard (11.4 cm) of light brown fleece
⅛ yard (11.4 cm) of black fleece
⅛ yard (11.4 cm) of dark brown fleece
2 black buttons

Before You Begin

When selecting your hoodie, it doesn't matter whether you pick one that has a zipper down the front or not. The embellishments will not interfere with a zipper.

Be sure to pick a hoodie size that leaves a little length in the arms so your child can place his or her fingers into a hidden pocket in the cuff and paw at any aggressors.

Matching sweatpants are nice but not necessary to complete the outfit.

Instructions

1 Cut two Snout pieces from light brown fleece using the Bear template. With right sides together, sew along the edge, leaving a 1-inch (2.5 cm) opening as marked on the template. Turn the snout right side out.

2 Place the snout so that it overlaps the edge of the hood by 1½ to 2 inches (3.8 to 5.1 cm). Eventually, the unsewn opening in the snout will be covered up by the nose piece, so be sure the opening is centered at the top of the snout. Attach it by hand-sewing under the snout along the front edge of the hood and along the top edge of the snout.

3 Cut two Nose pieces from black fleece using the template. With right sides together, sew along the edge, leaving a ½-inch (1.3 cm) opening. Turn the nose right side out and hand-sew the opening closed. Pin the nose at the top of the snout to cover the snout opening. Hand-sew the nose in place.

4 Cut four Ear pieces using the template, two with the pattern facing up and two with the pattern facing down, from dark brown fleece. Matching two pieces, place right sides together and sew along the curved edge of the ear, leaving the straight edge open as marked on the template. Turn the ear right side out. Repeat this step to create the other ear.

5 To give the ears dimension, fold them in half and sew along the straight edge. Pin and hand-sew the straight edge of the ears to the top of the hood in the desired location.

6 Just above the nose and snout, hand-sew the buttons in place for the eyes.

7 Cut two Tail pieces from dark brown fleece using the template. With right sides together, sew along the curved edge of the tail, leaving the straight edge open. Turn the tail right side out and hand-sew the straight edge to the back of the sweatshirt where desired.

Note: Place the tail a bit higher toward the lower back (instead of the seat area); this will be more comfortable for the bear when he or she sits down.

8 As mentioned in "Before You Begin," there are hidden pockets in the sleeve cuffs. In order to make them, cut two 1¾ x 3¾-inch (4.4 x 9.5 cm) rectangles from dark brown fleece. Figure out where the top of the cuff is—or where your little bear cub's fingers will fit into the pocket once the sweatshirt is on. Pin the rectangle in place there. Turn the sweatshirt right side out and hand-sew the rectangle in place. Repeat for the other sleeve.

9 Cut two Large Pads and eight Small Pads from light brown fleece using the template. Hand-sew the pads on the underside of the sleeves as shown in the photo above.

I love baby outfits that come fully equipped with bear ears. I've seen the ears on the hoods of teens, too. This outfit could be made in pastels for tiny tots or in bright, bold colors for older bear cubs.

Ladybug

tools & materials

Basic Sewing Tool Kit (page 14)
Ladybug Template (page 115)
Red hooded sweatshirt
¼ yard (22.9 cm) of black fleece
Scrap of black tulle
Scrap of red tulle
2 large black pom-poms

Before You Begin

When selecting your hoodie, pick one that has a zipper down the front because there is an embellishment along the zipper. If you aren't able to find a zippered hoodie, omit the tulle embellishment and add a few extra spots to the front of the sweatshirt.

To create a complementary tulle tutu that your little ladybug will love, turn to page 34.

Instructions

1 Measure the length from the sweatshirt's front neckline to the top of the pockets. Multiply this measurement by 3, and cut two 4-inch-wide (10.2 cm) black tulle strips this length. (For example, on the sweatshirt shown, the neckline to the top of the pocket measured 8 inches [20.3 cm]: 8 x 3 = 24 inches [61 cm] of black tulle were needed for a full ruffle.)

2 Place one strip of black tulle on top of the other and fold them in half lengthwise so the strips are now 2 inches (5.1 cm) wide. You can create a ruffle by basting along the folded edge and sliding the tulle down a bit on the thread. Once you adjust the tulle to the length that will fit between the neckline and the pocket, place the fold along the sweatshirt's zipper stitching line and pin it in place. Attach the tulle by hand-sewing it with a matching color of thread. Repeat this step for the other side of the zipper.

3 Repeat step 2, but this time, use red tulle that is 3 inches (7.6 cm) wide; when folded it will be 1½ inches (3.8 cm) wide. After creating this ruffle, hand-sew the folded edge along the same seam where you sewed the black tulle. After the stitching is complete, separate the layers to create a full ruffle.

4 Cut Spot pieces from the black fleece using the Ladybug template; the number depends upon how spotted you would like your Ladybug. Pin the spots randomly around the sweatshirt and hand-sew around their edges to secure them in place.

5 To create the antennas, cut two 3 x 6-inch (7.6 x 15.2 cm) rectangles from black fleece. Roll one up from the short end like a sleeping bag and stitch along the edge to keep the fleece from unrolling. Hand-sew a large pom-pom to one end and sew the other end to the top of the hood about 1 to 2 inches (2.5 to 5.1 cm) from the centerline. Repeat the rolling and sewing instructions to create and attach the second antenna.

Frog

Frog

tools & materials

Basic Sewing Tool Kit (page 14)

Frog Templates (page 112)

Kelly green hooded sweatshirt

Scrap of white fleece

¼ yard (22.9 cm) of Kelly green fleece

¼ yard (22.9 cm) of yellow fleece

¼ yard (22.9 cm) of green fleece

Polyester fiberfill

2 black beads, 6 or 8 mm in diameter

Washable fabric glue

6 Kelly green pom-poms, 1 inch (2.5 cm) in diameter

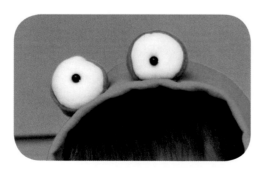

Before You Begin

When selecting your hoodie, it doesn't matter whether you pick one that has a zipper down the front or not. The embellishments will not interfere with a zipper. Matching sweatpants are nice but not necessary to complete the outfit.

Instructions

1 Cut two Eye pieces out of white fleece using the Frog template. Loosely baste around the outer edge of the circle and pull the thread to create a pouch. Stuff a small amount of polyester fiberfill in the pouch; cinch it shut and stitch the opening closed. Repeat these sewing instructions for the second eye.

2 Place a black bead on the center of the eye and pass the needle and thread from the back of the eyeball to the front to catch the bead. Repeat to ensure the bead is secure. Pull the thread tight so that the bead sinks slightly into the eye. Repeat these sewing instructions for the second eye.

3 Cut two Eyelid pieces out of Kelly green fleece using the template. Apply some washable fabric glue near the edge of the eyelid on the wrong side of the fleece; this will ensure the lid doesn't pop off the eye over time. Wrap the straight edge of the fleece around the eye and secure with pins. Let the glue dry. Baste around the curved edge of the eyelid as marked on the template. Pull the thread just as you did to create the eyeball in step 1. Stitch the eyelid in place on the eye. Repeat for the second eye.

4 Attach the eyes to the top of the hood as desired. The eyes on the costume shown are sewn to a seam encircling the front edge of the hood. There is about 1 inch (2.5 cm) in between the eyes.

5 Cut three Large Spots and six Small Spots from yellow fleece using the template. Hand-sew the spots in small groupings wherever you desire.

6 Cut four Hand pieces out of dark green fleece using the template. Match two with right sides together and machine-sew along all edges as marked on the template, leaving the long straight edge open. Turn the hand right side out and topstitch along the edges just sewn. Repeat these sewing instructions to create the second hand. Hand-sew a green pom-pom on each fingertip. Hand-sew the hands on the outside of the cuff, centering them on top of each wrist.

Jack-o'-Lantern

tools & materials

Basic Sewing Tool Kit (page 14)

Jack-o'-Lantern Templates (page 113)

Orange hooded sweatshirt

¼ yard (22.9 cm) of black fleece

Scrap of brown fleece

Scrap of dark green fleece

1 pipe cleaner (any color)

Polyester fiberfill

Before You Begin

When selecting your hoodie, pick one that does not have a zipper down the front because it can distort the face of the Jack-o'-Lantern. Matching sweatpants are nice but not necessary to complete the outfit.

Instructions

1 You can build your own jack-o'-lantern with the templates provided. Select which features you would like your jack-o'-lantern to have. Cut two Eye pieces, one Nose piece, and one Mouth piece from black fleece using the Jack-o'-Lantern templates. Arrange the face pieces on the front of the sweatshirt and pin them in place. Note that the mouth may have to go on the pocket. Hand-stitch around each piece to secure it in place.

2 Cut one Stem Top and one Stem Base from brown fleece using the templates. With right sides together, sew the short ends of the stem base together, creating a tube. With the right side of both the Stem Top and the Stem Base facing in, place the Stem Top on one end of the tube. Pin and sew them together. Turn the stem right side out and set it aside.

3 Cut two Leaf pieces from dark green fleece using the template, one with the pattern facing up and one with the pattern facing down. With right sides together, sew around the leaf, leaving the section open that is marked on the template. Turn the leaf right side out and hand-sew the opening closed. Machine-sew three decorative stitching lines on the leaf as shown on the template. Set the leaf aside.

4 To create the Jack-o'-Lantern's tendril, cut one ⅝-inch-wide (1.6 cm) piece of green fleece the length of the pipe cleaner. Fold the fleece in half lengthwise with the pipe cleaner in the center and stitch along all open edges. Wrap the tendril around your finger to create a spiral. Set the tendril aside.

5 Hand-sew the leaf to the center top of the hood. Loosely stuff the stem with polyester fiberfill. Gather the bottom of the stem, hand-sew it closed, and then sew it to the base of the leaf. Sew the tendril to the base of the stem to complete the Jack-o'-Lantern.

Princess

Princess

tools & materials

Basic Sewing Tool Kit (page 14)

Adding Capes Figures (page 15)

Pink hooded sweatshirt

Purple fleece:

    ½ yard (45.7 cm) for sizes 2T–3T

    ¾ yard (68.6 cm) for size 4T/XS

    1 yard (91.4 cm) for sizes S–M

    1¼ yards (114.3 cm) for sizes L–XL

2 yards (1.8 m) of purple crocheted headband ribbon

1 to 3 rolls of pink tulle (see A Note About Tulle at right)

1 to 3 rolls of purple tulle

Large piece of cardboard

2 yards (1.8 m) of purple grosgrain ribbon, ⅝ inch (1.6 cm) wide

Lighter

A Note About Tulle

Tulle often comes in 25-yard (22.9 m) rolls. Depending on the size of your skirt and the desired fullness, you'll need to purchase 25 to 75 yards (22.9 to 68.6 m) each of pink and purple tulle for your Princess costume.

Before You Begin

When selecting your hoodie, pick one without a zipper in front; the embellishments sewn onto the sweatshirt would interfere with a zipper. Leggings are recommended to complete this outfit.

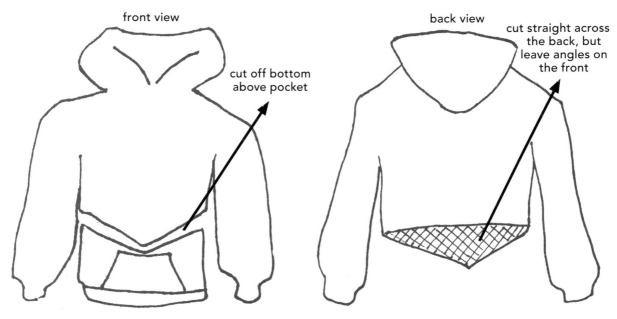

front view

back view

cut off bottom
above pocket

cut straight across
the back, but
leave angles on
the front

figure 1

Instructions

1 On the front side of the sweatshirt, just above the pocket, cut the bottom of the sweatshirt off by making two angled cuts toward the outside seams. Then cut straight across the back of the sweatshirt (figure 1).

2 Pin the roll of crocheted headband ribbon around the waist of the sweatshirt; start at the point of the V on the front and end there, too. Make sure you provide enough ribbon so you can overlap it as shown in the photo on page 62. Trim off any excess. Make sure that the bottom row of holes is hanging below the sweatshirt material so the tulle can be looped through. Machine-sew the crocheted ribbon through the middle onto the sweatshirt.

3 Decide what length you would like the skirt to be: knee length, mid-calf, tea length, or ankle length. Have the child try on the sweat-shirt and measure from the bottom of the attached waistband to the desired length of the skirt.

4 The easiest way to cut uniform pieces of tulle from a roll is to wrap the tulle around a piece of cardboard that is cut to the desired length. When all of the tulle is wrapped, make one cut anywhere across the wrapping. You now have tulle double the desired length, which is perfect because it will be folded in half. Cut one roll at a time in both pink and purple; don't cut more from the other rolls until you know you need it. (For more information on cutting tulle for a tutu, see the Tutu-torial on page 34.)

5 Fold a strip of tulle in half, creating a loop. At the center point on the front of the sweatshirt, insert the loop through a hole from the back of the crocheted waistband to the front. Bring the ends of the tulle up through the loop and gently pull to create a knot (figure 2). Repeat this knotting around the entire waistband, creating a pattern of three strips of pink followed by three strips of purple tulle.

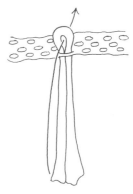

figure 2

6 Refer to the chart below and cut two lengths of grosgrain ribbon to use as ties to cinch the waist. Sew one end of each ribbon to each side of the outfit on the waistband. To prevent the ribbon from fraying, carefully wave a flame from a lighter near each end until it melts slightly.

Size	Length of Ribbon (cut 2)
2T–3T	16 inches (40.6 cm)
4T/XS	20 inches (50.8 cm)
S–M	24 inches (61 cm)
L–XL	28 inches (71.1 cm)

7 For the cape, cut the purple fleece to the following measurements, depending on what size sweatshirt you have:

Size	Fleece Size
2T–3T	½ yard (45.7 cm) square
4T/XS	¾ yard (68. 6 cm) square
S–M	1 yard (91.4 cm) square
L–XL	1¼ yards (114.3 cm) square

8 You will be hand-sewing the cape onto the sweatshirt, so grab your needle and thread. Fold the cape in half to find the middle. At this center point, begin pinning the cape to the middle of the back neck of the sweatshirt, under the hood. You will be folding the material under in 1-inch (2.5 cm) folds to give the cape some fullness (see Adding Capes figures, page 15). I ended the material before it reached the front of the costume so that the cape is always parted a bit. It really doesn't matter how you sew on the cape as long as it looks uniform on both sides and stays on for the long haul.

Make the Crown on page 63 to give your Princess some royal headgear!

Crown

tools & materials

Basic Sewing Tool Kit (page 14)
Crown Template (page 107)
¼ yard (22.9 cm) of gold fleece
4 button jewels (optional)

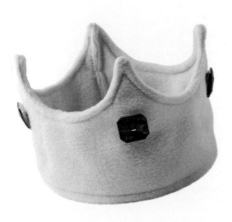

Before You Begin

The wonderful thing about working with fleece is that it stretches, which is a great quality for this one-size-fits-all crown!

Instructions

1 Cut two Crown pieces from gold fleece using the template. With right sides together, sew along the top curved edges and the straight bottom edge as marked on the template. Turn the crown right side out.

2 Fold the crown in half so the short ends line up. Machine-sew the ends together and turn the crown once again so the raw edges are on the inside.

3 Topstitch along the curved edges and along the bottom edge as marked on the template.

4 Leave the crown jewel free to complement your Prince's costume (page 64), or sew jewel buttons to it for your little Princess (page 59).

Prince

tools & materials

Basic Sewing Tool Kit (page 14)
Prince Template (page 118)
Adding Capes Figures (page 15)
Royal blue hooded sweatshirt
Red fleece:
¾ yard (68.6 cm) for sizes 2T–3T
1 yard (91.4 cm) for size 4T/XS
1¼ yards (114.3 cm) for sizes S–M
1½ yards (137 cm) for sizes L–XL

Before You Begin

When selecting your hoodie, it doesn't matter whether you pick one that has a zipper down the front or not. The embellishments will not interfere with a zipper. Matching sweatpants are nice but not necessary to complete the outfit.

Instructions

1 For the cape, cut the red fleece to the following measurements, based on what size sweatshirt you have. Set the fleece for the cape aside to use in step 4.

Sweatshirt Size	Fleece for the Cape
2T–3T	½ yard square (45.7 cm)
4T/XS	¾ yard square (68. 6 cm)
S–M	1 yard square (91.4 cm)
L–XL	1¼ yards square (114.3 cm)

2 Lay the sweatshirt out flat. Find the fold on the upper edge of each sleeve, directly across from the underarm seam. Along that fold, about 2 inches (5.1 cm) from the shoulder for sizes 2T to 4T/XS and 3 inches (7.6 cm) from the shoulder for all other sizes, make a cut with your scissors that is 4½ inches (11.4 cm) long for sizes 2T to 4T/XS or 6 inches (15.2 cm) for all other sizes. Halfway between this cut and the seam on the underside of the arm, make another cut on the front of the sleeve. Just as you did for the front of the sleeve, make a cut halfway between the seam and the first cut on the back of the sleeve (see figure 1). Repeat these cutting instructions for the other sleeve.

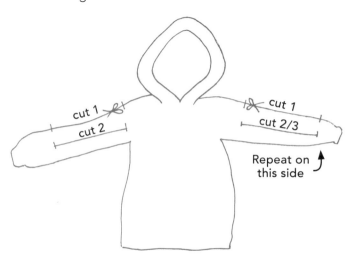

figure 1

3 Cut six Sleeve Embellishments from red fleece using the Prince template. Turn the sweatshirt inside out and pin each embellishment to one of the cuts, matching up the edges. Machine-sew along each edge. Turn the sweatshirt right side out and tack the ends of each point together.

4 Now you'll hand-sew the cape onto the sweatshirt, so grab your needle and thread. Fold the cape in half to find the middle. At this center point, begin pinning the cape to the middle of the back neck of the sweatshirt under the hood. You will be folding the material under in 1-inch (2.5 cm) folds to give the cape some fullness (see Adding Capes figures, page 15). I ended the material before it reached the front of the costume so that the cape is always parted a bit. It really doesn't matter how you sew on the cape as long as it looks uniform on both sides and stays on for the long haul.

Top off your Prince's costume with the Crown on page 63.

Scarecrow

Scarecrow

tools & materials

Basic Sewing Tool Kit (page 14)

Navy blue hooded sweatshirt

Brown sweatpants

¼ yard (22.9 cm) of yellow fleece

Scrap of brown fleece

Scrap of navy blue fleece

Light blue yarn

Yarn needle that can pass through the fleece and sweatshirt material

Rubber gloves

Before You Begin

When selecting your hoodie, it doesn't matter whether you pick one that has a zipper down the front or not. The embellishments will not interfere with the zipper.

Instructions

1 Using the self-healing mat, rotary cutter, and grid, cut the yellow fleece into a long strip 4 inches (10.2 cm) wide. Cut it into 1-inch (2.5 cm) pieces for the straw (figure 1). Depending on what size Scarecrow you are making and how full you would like the straw, you will need approximately 35 to 60 strips of straw.

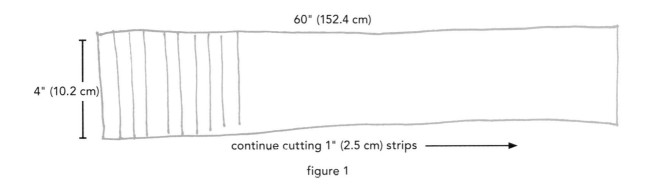

60" (152.4 cm)

4" (10.2 cm)

continue cutting 1" (2.5 cm) strips ⟶

figure 1

2 Hand-sew the straw pieces onto the sweat-shirt in small groupings. Stack two or three strips and angle them in different ways so they have some randomness, but keep one end of the bunch together (figure 2). Turn the sweatshirt inside out and begin sewing the straw bunches to the waistband seam. I left 1 to 2 inches (2.5 to 5.1 cm) between each grouping of "straw" as I worked around the waistband.

hand sew top to seamline

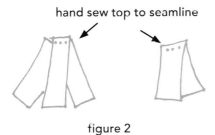

figure 2

3 Using the self-healing mat, rotary cutter, and grid, cut the remaining yellow fleece into a long strip 2½ inches (6.4 cm) wide. Cut this strip into more 1-inch (2.5 cm) straw pieces for the pants; these are just slightly shorter so your little Scarecrow doesn't trip. Depending on what size Scarecrow you are making and how full you would like the straw, you will need approximately 20 to 45 strips. Turn the pants inside out and begin sewing these straw pieces to the seam at the bottom of the sweatpants.

4 Cut two 3-inch (7.6 cm) squares from the scrap of brown fleece and one 3-inch (7.6 cm) square from the scrap of navy blue fleece. Hand-sew these patches to the outfit wherever you desire. I placed the brown patches on the blue sweatshirt and the blue patch on the brown pants for contrast. Using the yarn and a yarn needle, make a couple of decorative stitches on every side of each patch. I found that rubber gloves are the way to go when sewing with the yarn and the heavier needle; they will save your fingertips and provide grip to make the process go quicker.

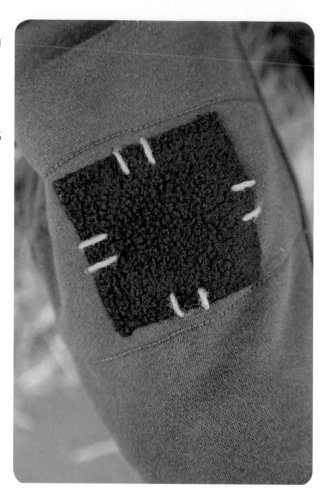

Don't be discouraged if birds don't fly away in terror of your little guy in this one! He'll be too cute to scare anything!

Dinosaur

Dinosaur

tools & materials

Basic Sewing Tool Kit (page 14)
Dinosaur Templates (page 108)
Green hooded sweatshirt
¼ yard (22.9 cm) of blue fleece
⅛ yard (11.4 cm) of white fleece
Polyester fiberfill

Before You Begin

When selecting your hoodie, it doesn't matter whether you pick one that has a zipper down the front or not. The embellishments will not interfere with a zipper. Matching sweatpants are nice but not necessary to complete the outfit.

Instructions

1 Determine how many scales are needed for your dinosaur by measuring the length of the sweatshirt starting at the top of the hood (preferably ½ to 1 inch [1.3 to 2.5 cm] from the front edge of the hood), going down the center of the back, and ending at the start of the waist ribbing. Once sewn, each scale is about 3 inches (7.6 cm) in length for sizes 2T to S, or 4 inches (10.2 cm) in length for the larger sizes. Divide this measurement by 3 for sizes 2T to S or by 4 for the larger sizes. The result is how many scales you need to make.

2 Cut two Scale pieces from blue fleece using the Dinosaur template. With right sides together, sew along the curved edges, leaving the straight edge open as marked on the template. Turn the scale right side out and topstitch along the curved edge just sewn. Loosely fill the scale with fiberfill. Repeat this step for each scale.

3 Mark the centerline of both the hood and the back of the sweatshirt. Hand-sew the first scale to the top of the hood ½ to 1 inch (1.3 to 2.5 cm) back from the front edge. Continue sewing the rest of the scales along this line and down the back. (The scales will butt against each other.)

4 Cut two Tooth pieces from white fleece using the template. With right sides together, sew along the curved edges, leaving the straight edge open as marked on the template. Turn the tooth right side out and topstitch along the just-sewn curved edge. Repeat this step seven more times to create a total of eight teeth.

5 Lay the sweatshirt out flat to find the outer edge of the right sleeve. Mark this fold. Hand-sew the first tooth on this line close to the start of the wrist ribbing. Continue attaching three more teeth along the fold line going toward the shoulder, with the teeth butting against each other.

6 On the left arm, sew the teeth onto the bottom edge of the sleeve along the seam. Start the first tooth close to the wrist ribbing and continue attaching the remaining three teeth going toward the underarm. The lucky wearer can now take a big dinosaur chomp using his or her arms (figure 1)!

figure 1

Scales are cool ... but, teeth? Teeth rule.

Shark

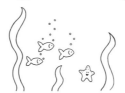

tools & materials

Basic Sewing Tool Kit (page 14)
Shark Templates (page 119)
Gray hooded sweatshirt
¼ yard (22.9 cm) of white fleece
¼ yard (22.9 cm) of gray fleece
2 black buttons
Batting

Before You Begin

When selecting your hoodie, it doesn't matter whether you pick one that has a zipper down the front or not. The embellishments will not interfere with a zipper. Matching sweatpants are nice but not necessary to complete the outfit.

Instructions

1 Cut 16 Tooth pieces from white fleece using the Shark template. Match two pieces with right sides together and machine-sew the two curved sides, leaving the straight edge open as marked on the template. Turn the tooth right side out and topstitch along the two edges just sewn. Repeat this step for the other seven teeth.

2 Pin the straight edges of the teeth to the inside of the hood, ¾ inch (1.9 cm) in from the outer edge, or along any available seam line. Start by centering the two front teeth, then work your way out, keeping the edges touching. Hand-sew each tooth in place. Remember that sweatshirt hood sizes may vary; if you find that eight teeth do not fit, just leave the last two off. Also, if you are making a sweatshirt with enough space and you would prefer to have more teeth, feel free to whip up a few more and sew them on.

3 Sew a button on each side of the hood for the eyes.

4 Cut two Fin pieces from gray fleece using the template, one with the pattern facing up and one with the pattern facing down. With right sides together, sew along the two curved edges as marked on the template, leaving the straight edge open. Turn the fin right side out and topstitch along the two curved edges just sewn. Cut one more Fin piece from the batting using the template. Trim a small amount of batting to fit the fin. Keeping the batting flat, slide it inside the fin.

5 Find the point where the tip of the hood falls on the back of the sweatshirt; you will sew the fin on below this point. Making sure the fin is centered on the back, pin and hand-sew it in place.

Dragon

tools & materials

Basic Sewing Tool Kit (page 14)
Dragon Templates (pages 108-109)
Light green hooded sweatshirt
¼ yard (22.9 cm) of dark green fleece
¼ yard (22.9 cm) of light green fleece
Polyester fiberfill

Before You Begin

When selecting your hoodie, it doesn't matter whether you pick one that has a zipper down the front or not. The embellishments will not interfere with a zipper. Matching sweatpants are nice but not necessary to complete the outfit.

Instructions

1 Cut two Spot A pieces, two Spot B pieces, four Spot C pieces, and two Spot D pieces from the dark green fleece using the Dragon templates. Hand-sew these pieces onto the chest of the sweatshirt (figure 1).

2 Cut two Horn A pieces and eight Horn B pieces from the dark green fleece using the templates. Match both Horn A pieces with right sides together. Machine-sew around the curved edge, leaving the straight edge open as marked on the template. Turn the horn right side out and loosely stuff it with polyester fiberfill. Repeat the sewing instructions in this step for the Horn B pieces, creating four smaller horns. Set the Horns aside.

figure 1

3 Cut two Spot A pieces, three Spot B pieces, two Spot C pieces, and three Spot D pieces from the dark green fleece using the templates. Set the Spots aside.

4 Cut four Ear pieces from the light green fleece using the template. Match two ear pieces with right sides together and sew along the curved edges, leaving the straight edge open as marked on the template. Turn the ear right side out and fold the straight edge in half. Loosely hand-stitch the bottom of the ear together to secure the fold. Set the Ears aside.

5 Now it is time to pin and hand-sew each of the pieces prepared in steps 2, 3, and 4 to the hood. Follow the placement shown in figure 2 below.

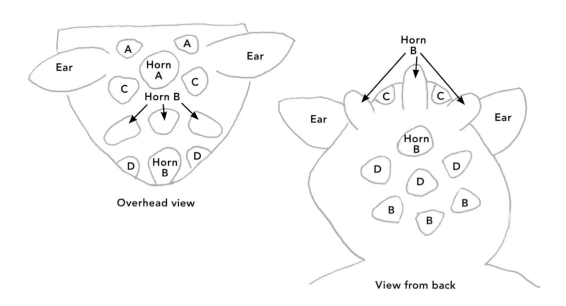

Overhead view

View from back

figure 2

6 Determine how many scales are needed for the dragon by measuring the length of the back of the sweatshirt starting at the neckline, continuing down the center of the back, and ending at the start of the waistband. Once sewn, each scale is around 3 inches (7.6 cm) in length or 4 inches (10.2 cm) if making sizes M to XL, so divide the length by 3 for the smaller sizes or 4 for the larger sizes. The result is how many scales you need to make.

7 Cut two Scale pieces from dark green fleece using the template. With right sides together, sew along the curved edges, leaving the straight edge open as marked on the template. Turn the scale right side out and topstitch along the just-sewn curved edge. Loosely fill the scale with fiberfill. Repeat this step for each scale. Hand-sew each scale to the sweatshirt down the center of its back.

8 Cut four Wing pieces, two with the pattern facing up and two with the pattern facing down, from dark green fleece using the template. Match two pieces, right sides together, and machine-sew along the edges marked on the template, leaving the short, straight edge open. Turn the wing right side out and topstitch along the top edges and down the center of the wing as marked. Repeat this step for the other wing. Hand-sew a wing to both sides of the scales at the location of the shoulder blades.

9 Cut two Tail pieces from dark green fleece, one with the pattern facing up and one with the pattern facing down, using the template. Match these two pieces with right sides together. Machine-sew along the edges as marked on the template, leaving the straight edge open. Turn the tail right side out and topstitch down the center of the tail as marked on the template. Hand-sew the tail onto the back of the sweatshirt below the lowest scale. (It's not stuffed, so it'll be comfortable for your child to sit on!)

Gingerbread Person

tools & materials

Basic Sewing Tool Kit (page 14)

Brown hooded sweatshirt

Brown sweatpants

White jumbo rickrack, 1½ inches (3.8 cm) wide (see "Before You Begin," at right, to calculate the amount needed)

3 large red buttons

Before You Begin

When selecting your hoodie, it doesn't matter whether you pick one that has a zipper down the front or not. The embellishments will not interfere with a zipper. Matching sweatpants are recommended to complete the look.

Because sweatshirts may vary from manufacturer to manufacturer, the amount of rickrack, or "frosting," required for this project will vary. To calculate how much you will need, measure around the edge of the hood, the ends of the arms, the ends of the legs, and the waist. Add 6 inches (15.2 cm) to this measurement because you will need to tuck the edges of the rickrack under for a finished edge.

Instructions

1 Sew the rickrack "frosting" on the sweatshirt by pinning it in place, tucking the excess edges underneath, and machine-sewing straight through the middle of the rickrack. Refer to the photo shown for the "frosting" placement.

Tips: Use your best judgment when deciding the exact placement of the rickrack "frosting" because your sweatshirt may have ribbing, seams, or decorative stitching. On the costume shown, the rickrack is stitched near the edge of the hood, above the ribbing around the ends of the sleeves, on the sweatshirt's waistband, and around the ankles of the sweatpants' legs.

If you have a hoodie with a zipper, wrap the rickrack around the waist, but be sure to tuck each end under on either side of the zipper. Your sweatshirt opens—make sure the frosting doesn't get in the way!

2 Hand-sew the three buttons down the center of the shirt above the pocket. If you have a zippered hoodie, sew the buttons onto the sweatshirt material on one side of the zipper. The zipper will still be able to pass behind the buttons.

Your Gingerbread Person is done — no need to bake!

It's physically impossible to wear this and not say, "Run, run as fast as you can, you can't catch me, I'm the Gingerbread Man!" Look for these outfits on the track at the next summer Olympics!

Knight

Knight

tools & materials

Basic Sewing Tool Kit (page 14)
Knight Templates (page 114)
Adding Capes Figures (page 15)
Gray hooded sweatshirt
¾ yard (68.6 cm) of gray fleece
¾ yard (68.6 cm) of red fleece

Before You Begin

When selecting your hoodie, it doesn't matter whether you pick one that has a zipper down the front or not. The embellishments will not interfere with a zipper. Matching sweatpants are nice but not necessary to complete the outfit.

Instructions

1 Using the Knight template, cut two Mask pieces from gray fleece, one with the pattern facing up and one with the pattern facing down. With right sides together, sew along the outer edges, leaving one short end open as shown. Turn the mask right side out and tuck the edges of the open end in. Topstitch along this side to secure the loose ends. Continue topstitching along the outer edge. Make three more stitching lines from the top of the mask to the bottom in the locations shown on the template. Attach the mask by tacking it to the front edge of the hood as shown on the template. Tack the sides of the mask to either side of the hood.

2 Cut a 1 x 16-inch (2.5 x 40.6 cm) strip of gray fleece. Starting at the short end, roll it like a sleeping bag so the right side is facing out. Sew along the loose end to keep it from unrolling. Place this roll on the very top of the hood and hand-sew the bottom edge to attach it.

3 Cut four Shoulder pieces from gray fleece using the template. Match two pieces with right sides together and machine-sew around the edges, leaving an opening as marked on the template. Turn the shoulder piece right side out and top-stitch around the outer edge, tucking in the loose edges. Repeat this step for the second shoulder piece. Fold these pieces of armor in half, wrap them around the top of the shoulders, and hand-sew them in place.

4 Cut four Wrist pieces from the gray fleece using the template, two with the pattern facing up and two with the pattern facing down. Match two pieces with right sides together and sew along the outer edges, leaving one of the short ends open as shown on the template. Turn the wrist piece right side out and topstitch around the outer edge, tucking in the loose edge. Fold the wrist piece in half, matching the angled edges. Machine-sew the two edges together between the two points marked on the template. Repeat to create the second wrist piece. Place the sweatshirt arms into the wrist pieces so that the bottom edges are around the wrists. If your sweatshirt has ribbing around the wrists, hand-sew the wrist pieces along the seam that connects the ribbing to the sweatshirt. If it has no ribbing, sew the wrist pieces along the edge of the sleeve.

5 For the cape, cut the red fleece to the measurements shown on the chart, depending on what size sweatshirt you are using. (Note: Cut the Cape and the Cowl lengthwise on the fabric.)

Sweatshirt Size	Fleece for Cape
2T–3T	¼ x ½ yard (22.9 x 45.7 cm)
4T–XS	½ x ¾ yard (45.7 x 68.6 cm)
S–M	½ x 1 yard (45.7 x 91.4 cm)
L–XL	½ x 1¼ yards (45.7 x 114.3 cm)

6 You will be hand-sewing the cape onto the sweatshirt, so grab your needle and thread. Fold the short end of the cape in half to find the middle. At this center point, begin pinning the cape to the middle back of the sweatshirt at the neck, under the hood. You will be folding the material under in 1-inch (2.5 cm) folds to give the cape some fullness (See Adding Capes figures, page 15). It will fit between the shoulder pieces.

7 The last step is to create a cowl for the knight; sometimes knights have part of their cape wrapped around their neck, which is represented by this piece. Cut a strip of red fleece 6 x 26 inches (15.2 x 66 cm) for sizes 2T to S, or 6 x 32 inches (15.2 x 81.3 cm) for sizes M to XL lengthwise on the fabric. Fold the strip with right sides together, matching up the short ends. Sew the two short ends together and turn the cowl right side out. Slip this piece over the head, around the neck, and under the hood.

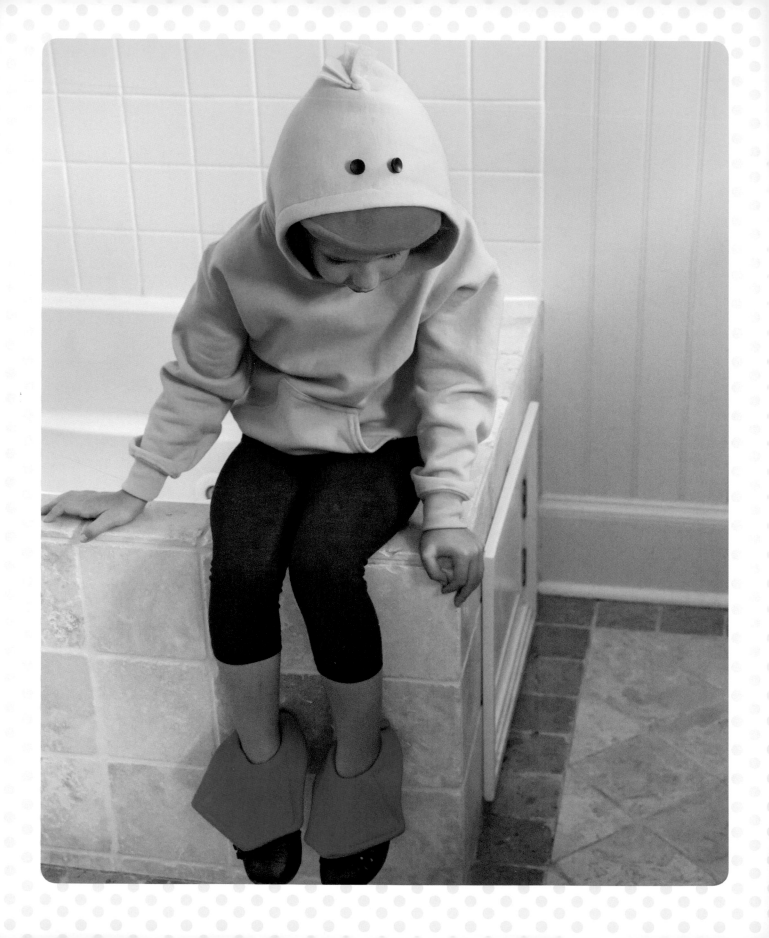

Ducky

tools & materials

Basic Sewing Tool Kit (page 14)
Ducky Template (page 109)
Golden yellow hooded sweatshirt
¼ yard (22.9 cm) of orange fleece
Scrap of golden yellow fleece
2 black buttons

Before You Begin

When selecting your hoodie, it doesn't matter whether you pick one that has a zipper down the front or not. The embellishments will not interfere with a zipper. Matching sweatpants are nice but not necessary to complete the outfit.

Instructions

1 Cut two Bill pieces from the orange fleece using the Ducky template. With right sides together, sew along the curved edge as marked on the template. Turn the bill right side out and topstitch along the curved edge just sewn.

2 Tuck about ¾ inch (1.9 cm) of the bill under the edge of the hood, with the curved edge facing out like the brim on a baseball cap. Hand-sew along the straight edge to attach it. There may be a seam line inside the hood that you can follow.

3 Center and attach the buttons on the top of the hood about 1½ inches (3.8 cm) from the front edge, or where desired.

4 Cut two 1 x 5-inch (2.5 x 12.7 cm) strips from the golden yellow fleece. With the two strips stacked together, tie a knot in the center to create a small tuft of hair for the Ducky. Hand-sew the tuft to the top of the hood.

The Ducky Feet on page 90 are just what you need to put the finishing touch on this outfit.

Ducky Feet

tools & materials

Basic Sewing Tool Kit (page 14)
Ducky Feet Template (page 110)
¼ yard (22.9 cm) of orange fleece
1½-inch (3.8 cm) piece of hook-and-loop tape, ¾ inch (1.9 cm) wide

Before You Begin

Select the template size of Ducky Feet to make based on the shoe size.

Ducky Template Size	Shoe Size
XS	5–9
S	10–1
M	2-5
L	5-7

Instructions

1 Using the template, cut four Ducky Feet from the orange fleece, two with the pattern facing up and two with the pattern facing down. Match two together with right sides facing. Sew along the outer edge, starting at point A and ending at point B as marked on the template. Turn the foot right side out.

2 Fold the open edge in ¼ inch (6 mm) and topstitch along the opening to secure it shut.

3 Topstitch the webbing marks on the top of the foot.

4 Repeat steps 1 through 3 to make the second Ducky Foot.

5 Cut two ¾-inch (1.9 cm) squares of hook-and-loop tape, one set for each foot. Center the hook-and-loop tape on each end of the back, one piece on the top of the foot piece and one on the underside, and sew them in place.

Superhero

Superhero

tools & materials

Basic Sewing Tool Kit (page 14)

Superhero Templates (pages 120-121)

Navy blue hooded sweatshirt

Lime green fleece:

> ½ yard (45.7 cm) for sizes 2T–3T
>
> ¾ yard (68.6 cm) for size 4T/XS
>
> 1 yard (91.4 cm) for sizes S–M
>
> 1¼ yards (114.3 cm) for sizes L–XL

1 sheet of lime green stiffened craft felt, 9 x 12 inches (22.9 x 30.5 cm)

¼ yard (22.9 cm) of royal blue fleece

Washable fabric glue

Before You Begin

When selecting your hoodie, pick one that does not have a zipper down the front, which can distort the superhero emblem. Matching sweatpants are nice but not necessary to complete the outfit.

Instructions

1 Select the letter you will use from the Superhero Emblem Templates. Using the template, cut out the emblem from the lime green craft felt. Next cut the Emblem Background from royal blue fleece using the template. Apply fabric glue to the back of the Superhero Emblem and glue it to the front of the Emblem Background. Machine-sew around the outer edge of the green emblem to ensure it stays in place. After the glue dries, hand-sew the Emblem to the front of the sweatshirt, centered on the chest area.

2 Measure around the bottom of the sweat-shirt above the waistband but below the openings for the pocket. Using this measurement, cut a 2-inch-wide (5.1 cm) strip of royal blue fleece long enough to wrap around the bottom of the sweatshirt. Pin the strip just above the waistband, starting and ending with one end centered on the front of the pocket; the Belt Buckle will cover these raw edges. Hand-sew the strip in place, making sure not to sew the pocket shut.

3 Cut one Belt Buckle from lime green fleece using the template. Center this on the sweatshirt pocket, covering the belt strip's raw edges, and hand-sew it in place. (Be sure not to sew through the pocket.)

4 For the cape, cut the lime green fleece to the following measurements, depending on what size sweatshirt you have:

Size	Fleece Size
2T–3T	½ yard square (45.7 cm)
4T/XS	¾ yard square (68.6 cm)
S–M	1 yard square (91.4 cm)
L–XL	1¼ yards square (114.3 cm)

> Little boys everywhere can thank my husband that the painted sparkle underwear didn't make the final cut for this costume.

5 You will be hand-sewing the cape onto the sweatshirt, so grab your needle and thread. Fold the cape in half to find the middle. At this center point, begin pinning the cape to the middle of the back neck of the sweatshirt, under the hood. You will be folding the material under in 1-inch (2.5 cm) folds to give the cape some fullness (see Adding Cape figures, page 15). I ended my material before it reached the front of the costume so it is always parted a bit. It really doesn't matter how you sew on the cape as long as it looks uniform on both sides and stays on for the long haul.

Little Red Riding Hood

tools & materials for cape

Basic Sewing Tool Kit (page 14)

Red hooded sweatshirt (see "Before You Begin")

2 to 4 yards (1.8 to 3.7 m) of red ruffled ribbon

⅔ yard (61 cm) of black ribbon

1 hook and eye

Before You Begin

When selecting a hoodie, choose an oversized sweatshirt so there is enough material for the cape. As a general guideline, follow the chart below:

Clothing Size	Sweatshirt Size for Cape
2T–4T/XS	Youth XL–Adult S
S	Adult M
M	Adult L
L	Adult XL
XL	Adult XXL

It doesn't matter whether you select a hoodie with or without a zipper. The instructions below will tell you how to handle both. Leggings are recommended to complete this outfit.

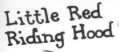

Cape Instructions

Cutting the Sweatshirt

1 If the hoodie has a zipper down the front, start by cutting it out. Cut alongside the zipper from the bottom of the sweatshirt ribbing up to the neck. (See blue dashed line on figure 1.)

If there is no zipper on the front of the sweatshirt, cut up through the center of the hoodie (on the front side only) from the bottom of the sweatshirt ribbing up to the neck. (See purple dashed line on figure 1.)

2 Cut the ribbing off the bottom of the sweatshirt. (See green dashed line on figure 1.)

3 To remove the pocket from the cape, make an angled cut along the front of the sweatshirt that just misses the corner of the pocket as shown in the diagram. Repeat this exact angle (only mirrored) on the other side. (See red dashed line on figure 1.) It is a good idea to blend the point that may be created at the bottom of the sweatshirt where the side seams are. Instead of a point, there should be a gradual curve that leads to the back of the cape.

4 To remove the arms, cut the sides of the sweatshirt up to the shoulders, being sure to cut some excess width off the sweatshirt. (See yellow dashed line on figure 1.) To allow for a smoother seam, cut a gradual curve at the shoulder to blend the point. You will also want to cut out the current seam for the top of the shoulders.

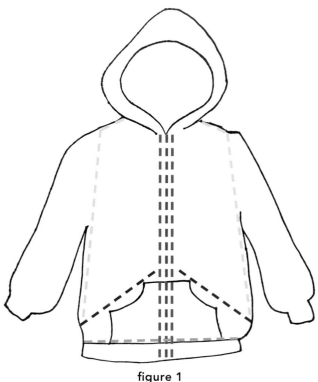

figure 1

Sewing the Cape

5 Turn the cape inside out and pin along the edges of the cape and its shoulders. Machine-sew along the edges.

6 Pin and sew the red ruffle ribbon along the edges of the cape to finish the edges. Start at the neckline where the cape meets the hood and follow the unfinished edge all the way down, around the back of the cape, and back up to the front on the other side, ending at the neckline once again.

7 Sew the hook and eye in place by the seam at the neck. Make a bow from the black ribbon and hand-sew it over one side of the hook and eye. When the cape is fastened, it should look like the bow is doing the work.

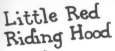

tools & materials for dress

White fitted T-shirt

2 yards (1.8 m) of black crocheted headband ribbon (often comes in a 2-yard [1.8 m] roll)

Large piece of cardboard

2 to 5 rolls of red tulle (see A Note About Tulle, below)

1 to 2 rolls of white tulle

⅔ yard (61 cm) of black ribbon, ¼ inch 6 mm) wide

Washable fabric glue

⅔ yard (61 cm) of black decorative ribbing

A Note About Tulle

Tulle often comes in 25-yard (22.9 m) rolls. Depending on the size of your skirt and the desired fullness, you'll need to purchase 50 to 125 yards (45.7 to 114.3 m) of red tulle and 25 to 50 yards (22.9 to 45.7 m) of white tulle for your Red Riding Hood costume.

Dress Instructions

1 Purchase a fitted T-shirt in the correct size for your child. Have her try on the shirt and mark under the bust, because you will be creating an empire waistline. Cut off the shirt 1 inch (2.5 cm) below the markings.

2 Pin the crocheted headband ribbon around the waist of the T-shirt, starting and ending at the center back. Make sure you provide enough overlap for the crocheted ribbon to look continuous, and trim off any excess. You also want to be sure that the bottom row of holes is hanging below the T-shirt material so the tulle can be looped through. Machine-sew the ribbon through its middle onto the T-shirt.

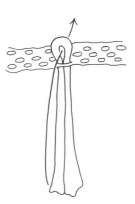

3 Decide what length you would like the skirt to be: knee length, mid-calf, tea length, or ankle length. Try the T-shirt on your Little Red Riding Hood once again and measure from the bottom of the attached waistband to the desired length.

4 The easiest way to cut many uniform pieces of tulle from a roll is to wrap the tulle around a piece of cardboard that is cut to the desired length. When all of the tulle is wrapped, make one cut anywhere across the wrapping. You now have tulle double the desired length, which is perfect because it will be folded in half. Cut one roll at a time in red and white; don't cut more from the other rolls until you know you need it. (For more information on cutting tulle, see the Tutu-torial on page 34.)

5 Fold a strip of white tulle in half, creating a loop. At the center point on the front of the T-shirt, insert the loop through a hole from the back of the crocheted waistband to the front. Bring the ends of the tulle up through the loop and gently pull to create a knot (figure 1). Move to the next hole and repeat this knotting to create a section of white tulle 6 to 9 inches (15.2 to 22.9 cm) wide at the center front of the dress for the apron look. Continue on either side of the white tulle and around the back with red tulle.

6 The final touch is to add ribbon on the front of the T-shirt. For sizes 2T to S, cut four 4-inch (10.2 cm) sections of ¼-inch-wide (6 mm) black ribbon; for sizes M to XL cut four 6-inch (15.2 cm) sections of ¼-inch-wide (6 mm) black ribbon. Place the scrap of cardboard in between the layers of the T-shirt and glue the ribbon in a crisscross pattern down the front. Cover the edges of the crisscrossed ribbon by gluing a piece of black ribbing to both sides. Make sure the ribbing goes from the edging of the neckline down to the crocheted waistband.

figure 1

After trying it on for the first time, my daughter couldn't take this outfit off. Beware of the many hours you'll now be required to play the big bad wolf.

Unicorn

tools & materials

Basic Sewing Tool Kit (page 14)

Unicorn Templates (page 122)

Dark pink hooded sweatshirt

½ yard (45.7 cm) of light pink fleece

⅛ yard (11.4 cm) of dark pink fleece

⅛ yard (11.4 cm) of light yellow fleece

Polyester fiberfill

Before You Begin

When selecting your hoodie, it doesn't matter whether you pick one that has a zipper down the front or not. The embellishments will not interfere with a zipper. Matching sweatpants are nice but not necessary to complete the outfit.

Instructions

1 Measure the length of the sweatshirt hood, starting at the center of its front edge to the nape of its neck. Cut two rectangles from light pink fleece the length of this measurement and 6 inches (15.2 cm) wide. Cut fringe 1 inch (2.5 cm) wide along each side of the rectangle, leaving the center ½ inch (1.3 cm) of each rectangle uncut. This will be the unicorn's mane.

2 Lining up the short ends of both pieces with the front edge of the hood, machine-sew the mane down the middle. To add some pizzazz, loosely knot two fringe pieces together. Continue randomly knotting as far back on the mane as desired.

3 Using the Unicorn template, cut two Ear pieces from the dark pink fleece and two Ear pieces from the light pink fleece. Place one dark pink Ear piece and one light pink Ear piece with right sides together. Sew along the two curved edges, leaving the straight edge open. Turn the ear right side out and topstitch along the curved edges just sewn as marked on the template. Repeat this step to create the second ear. Hand-sew the ears in place on both sides of the mane.

4 Cut one Horn piece from light yellow fleece using the template. As shown on the template, fold the Horn in half with right sides together and sew along the straight edge. Gently stuff fiberfill into the tip of the horn and continue stuffing it all the way down. Hand-sew the bottom edge of the horn into the mane about 1 inch (2.5 cm) from the front edge of the hood. Make sure the horn's seam is facing toward the back of the sweatshirt.

5 To create the grooves in the horn, bring a needle and knotted thread through at the seam at the bottom of the horn. Tightly twist the thread around the horn at an angle and make another knotlike stitch once you reach the seam. Continue twisting up around the horn, keeping the thread taut to create a groove. When you are approaching the top and are satisfied with the look of the grooves, secure the thread with a final knot.

6 To create the tail, cut a 6 x 20-inch (15.2 x 50.8 cm) rectangle from the light pink fleece. Fold the rectangle in half crosswise so you have a 6 x 10-inch (15.2 x 25.4 cm) rectangle. Cut 1-inch (2.5 cm) strips from the edge up to the fold, leaving 1 inch (2.5 cm) uncut in the center. Keep the fleece folded and roll the uncut end of the fleece like a sleeping bag, creating a long tassel for the tail. Hand-sew all layers of this roll in place and attach the tassel to the back of the sweatshirt near the top of the waistband.

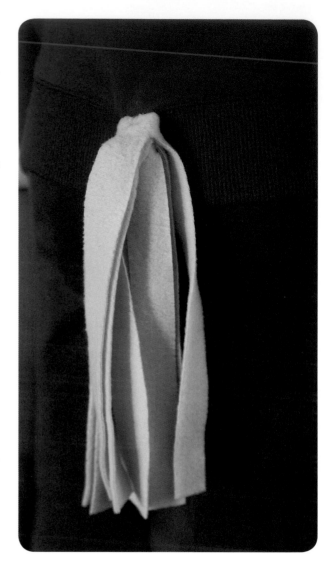

My finished unicorn just happened to be the current size my six-year-old son wears ... and I needed a model. It cost me $3 to get him to put it on. It was worth it to have that picture. It'll be perfect for his graduation party!

Fox

tools & materials

Basic Sewing Tool Kit (page 14)

Fox Templates (page 111)

Orange hooded sweatshirt

⅓ yard (30.5 cm) of orange fleece

¼ yard (22.9 cm) of off-white fleece

Scrap of black fleece

Before You Begin

When selecting your hoodie, it doesn't matter whether you pick one that has a zipper down the front or not. The embellishments will not interfere with a zipper. Matching sweatpants are nice but not necessary to complete the outfit.

Instructions

1 Cut two Ear pieces from orange fleece and two Ear pieces from off-white fleece using the Fox template. Cut two Ear Accents from black fleece. Place the wrong side of one piece of black fleece on top of the right side of one piece of orange fleece, matching the pointed tips together. Sew along the bottom curve of the black fleece, attaching it to the orange fleece. Repeat these sewing instructions for the second ear.

2 Take one orange/black ear piece and one off-white ear piece and match them with the right sides together. Sew along the curved edges of the ear, leaving the straight edge open as marked on the template. Turn the ear right side out and repeat this step for the second ear.

3 To make the ears look more realistic, fold one-third of each ear over lengthwise and hand-sew along the straight edge to secure it. Pin the ears on the hood at the angle you desire, and sew the straight edges of the ears on either side of the hood where desired.

4 Cut two Tail pieces from orange fleece and two Tail Tuft pieces from off-white fleece using the templates. Place the wrong side of one off-white piece on top of the right side of one piece of orange fleece, matching the pointed tips together. Sew along the zigzag edge of the off-white fleece, attaching it to the orange piece. Repeat these sewing instructions for the second side of the tail.

5 Match up and pin the orange/off-white tail pieces with right sides together. You may want to check to make sure the seams on the off-white tufts line up and pin them to keep them aligned when sewing. Sew along the curved edges of the tail, leaving the straight edge open as marked on the template. Turn the tail right side out. Topstitch along each curved edge up to the off-white tufts.

Note: There is no fiberfill stuffing in this tail to make sitting more comfortable!

6 Hand-sew the straight edge of the tail to the back of the sweatshirt where desired.

Templates
Bear

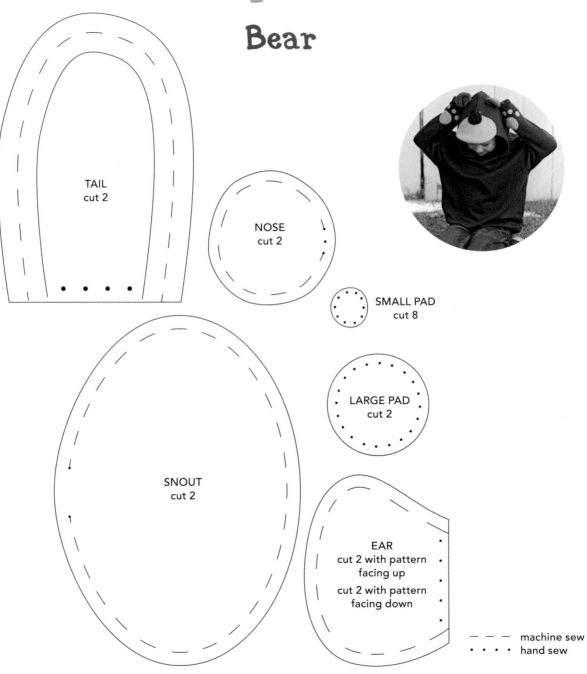

TAIL
cut 2

NOSE
cut 2

SMALL PAD
cut 8

LARGE PAD
cut 2

SNOUT
cut 2

EAR
cut 2 with pattern
facing up

cut 2 with pattern
facing down

– – – machine sew
• • • • hand sew

Tail is at full size
Enlarge all other templates 200%

Bumblebee

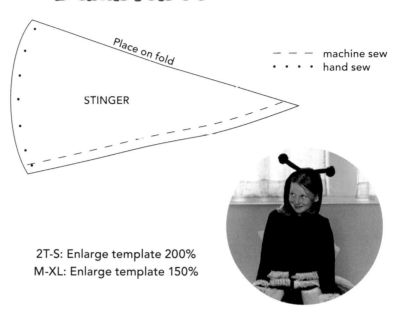

Place on fold

STINGER

– – – machine sew
• • • hand sew

2T-S: Enlarge template 200%
M-XL: Enlarge template 150%

Crown

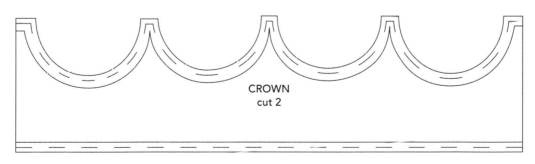

CROWN
cut 2

– – – machine sew
——— topstitch

Enlarge template 400%

Dinosaur

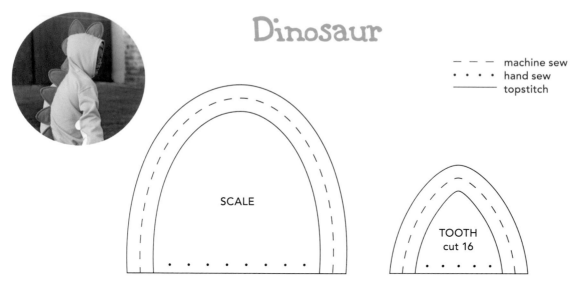

machine sew
hand sew
topstitch

SCALE

TOOTH
cut 16

2T-S: Enlarge templates 150%
M-XL: Enlarge templates 200%

Dragon

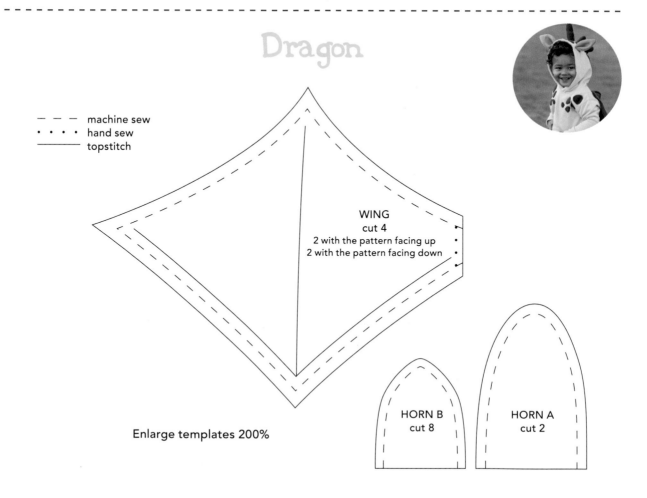

machine sew
hand sew
topstitch

WING
cut 4
2 with the pattern facing up
2 with the pattern facing down

Enlarge templates 200%

HORN B
cut 8

HORN A
cut 2

Dragon (continued)

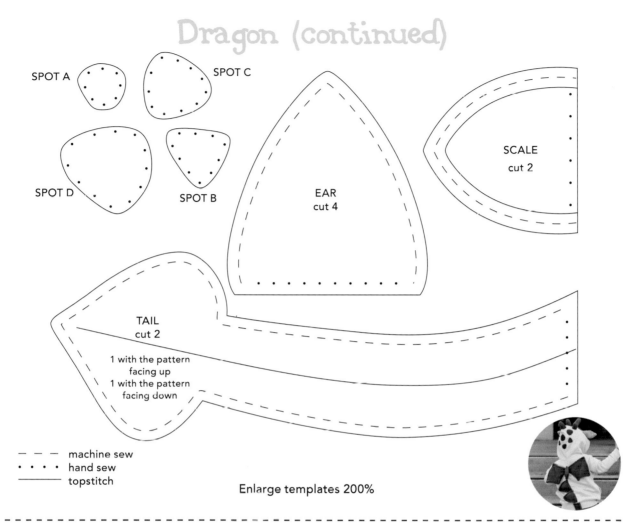

SPOT A

SPOT C

SPOT D

SPOT B

EAR
cut 4

SCALE
cut 2

TAIL
cut 2

1 with the pattern
facing up
1 with the pattern
facing down

– – – machine sew
• • • • hand sew
—— topstitch

Enlarge templates 200%

Ducky

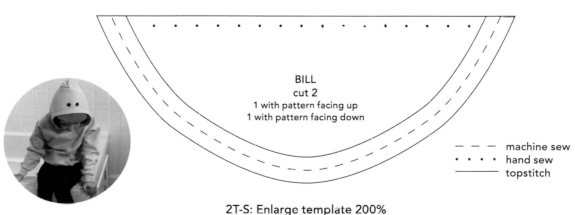

BILL
cut 2
1 with pattern facing up
1 with pattern facing down

– – – machine sew
• • • • hand sew
—— topstitch

2T-S: Enlarge template 200%
M-XL: Enlarge template 250 %

Ducky Feet

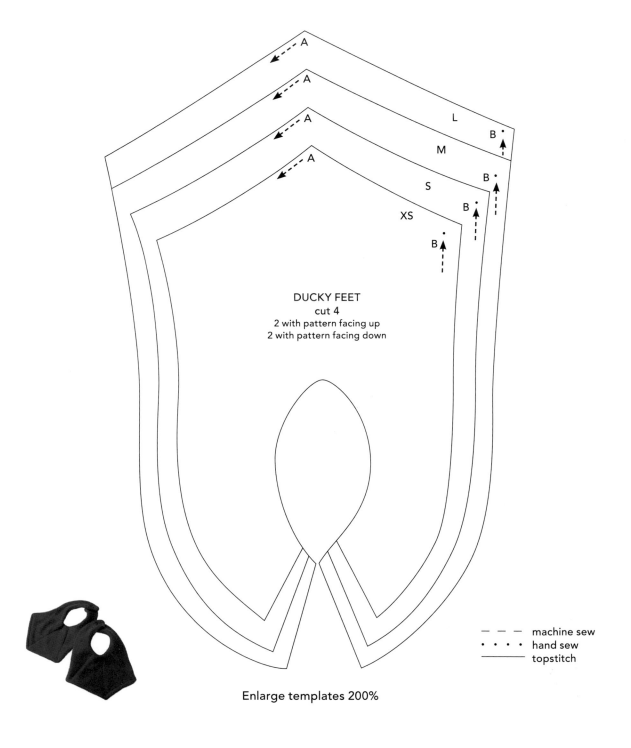

A

A

A

A

L

M

S

XS

B

B

B

B

DUCKY FEET
cut 4
2 with pattern facing up
2 with pattern facing down

– – – machine sew
• • • • hand sew
——— topstitch

Enlarge templates 200%

Fairy

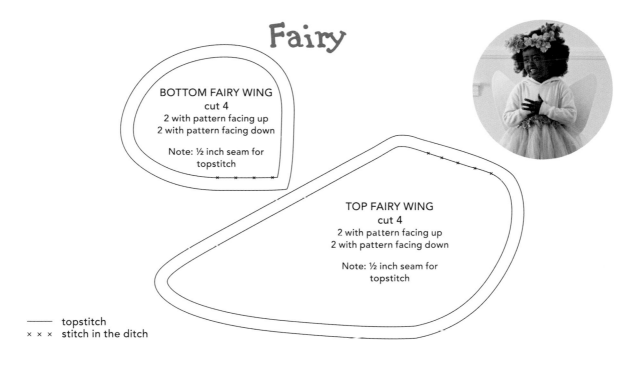

BOTTOM FAIRY WING
cut 4
2 with pattern facing up
2 with pattern facing down

Note: ½ inch seam for
topstitch

TOP FAIRY WING
cut 4
2 with pattern facing up
2 with pattern facing down

Note: ½ inch seam for
topstitch

—— topstitch
× × × stitch in the ditch

Enlarge templates 400%

Fox

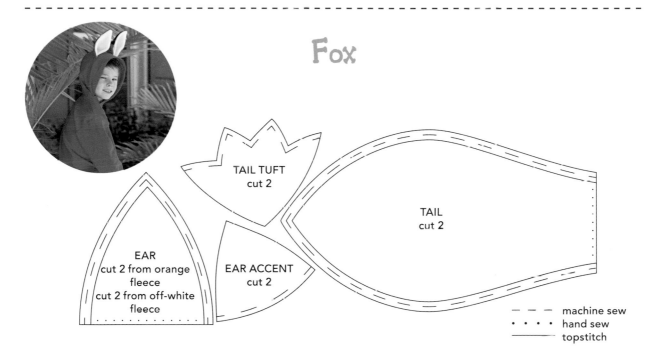

TAIL TUFT
cut 2

EAR
cut 2 from orange
fleece
cut 2 from off-white
fleece

EAR ACCENT
cut 2

TAIL
cut 2

– – – machine sew
• • • • hand sew
—— topstitch

2T-S: Enlarge templates 300%
M-XL: Enlarge templates 400%

Frog

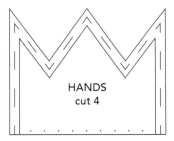

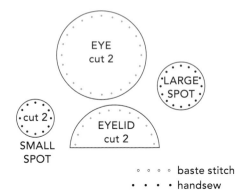

HANDS
cut 4

EYE
cut 2

LARGE SPOT

cut 2
SMALL SPOT

EYELID
cut 2

– – – machine sew
——— topstitch
· · · · handsew

∘ ∘ ∘ baste stitch
· · · · handsew

For Hands:
2T-S: Enlarge template 300%
M-XL: Enlarge template 400%
Enlarge all other templates 400% for all sizes

Gnome/Wizard

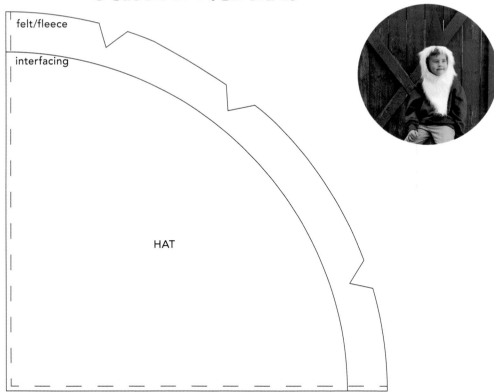

felt/fleece

interfacing

HAT

2T-S: Enlarge template 300%
M-XL: Enlarge template 400%

– – – machine sew

Jack-o'-Lantern

EYES - Choose one eye, and cut 1 with pattern facing up, cut 1 with pattern facing down

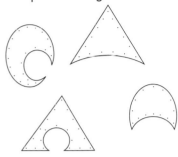

MOUTHS - Choose one mouth, and cut 1

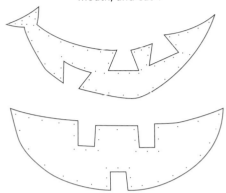

NOSES - Choose one nose, and cut 1

STEM BASE
cut 1

STEM TOP
cut 1

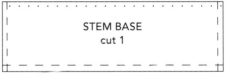
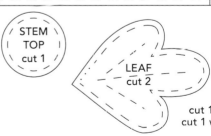

LEAF
cut 2

cut 1 with pattern facing up
cut 1 with pattern facing down

– – – machine sew
· · · · hand sew
——— topstitch

For Eyes, Noses, and Mouths:
2T-4T: Enlarge templates 300%
S-XL: Enlarge templates 400%

Stem Base, Stem Top, and Leaf: Enlarge 400% for all sizes

Knight

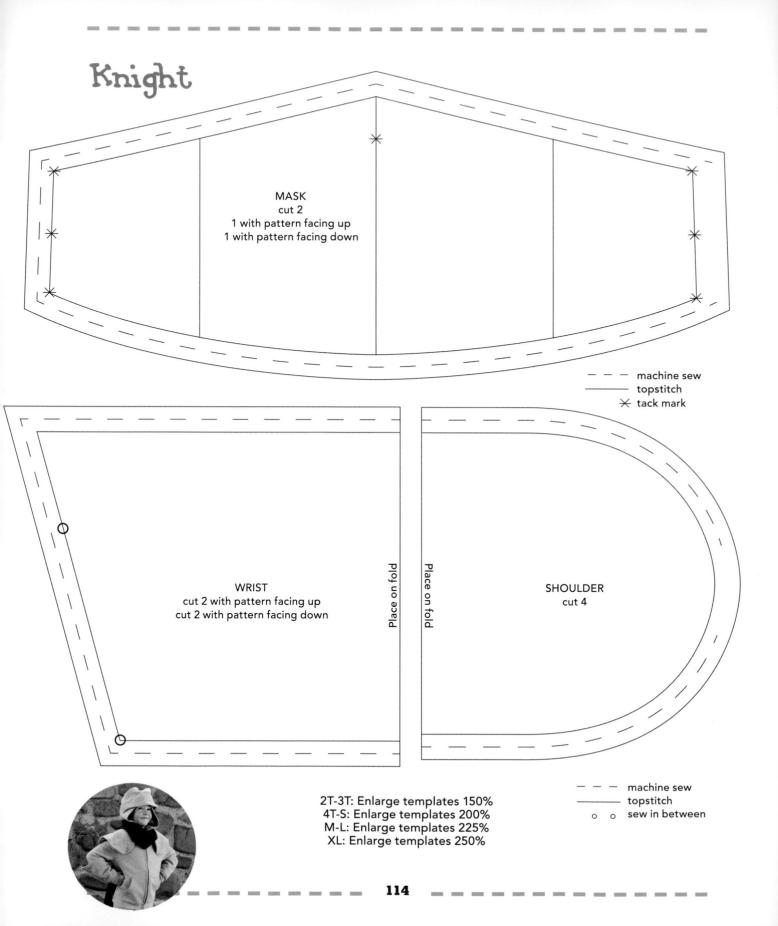

MASK
cut 2
1 with pattern facing up
1 with pattern facing down

- - - machine sew
——— topstitch
✳ tack mark

WRIST
cut 2 with pattern facing up
cut 2 with pattern facing down

Place on fold

Place on fold

SHOULDER
cut 4

- - - machine sew
——— topstitch
o o sew in between

2T-3T: Enlarge templates 150%
4T-S: Enlarge templates 200%
M-L: Enlarge templates 225%
XL: Enlarge templates 250%

Ladybug

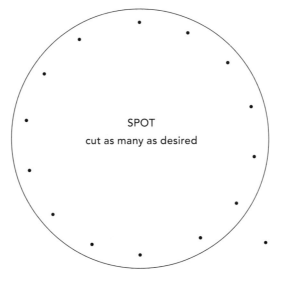

SPOT

cut as many as desired

• • • handsew

Template is at full size

Magic Wand

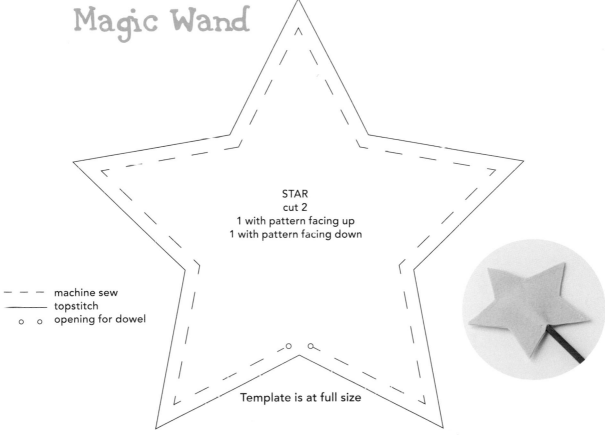

STAR
cut 2
1 with pattern facing up
1 with pattern facing down

– – – machine sew
——— topstitch
o   o   opening for dowel

Template is at full size

Monster

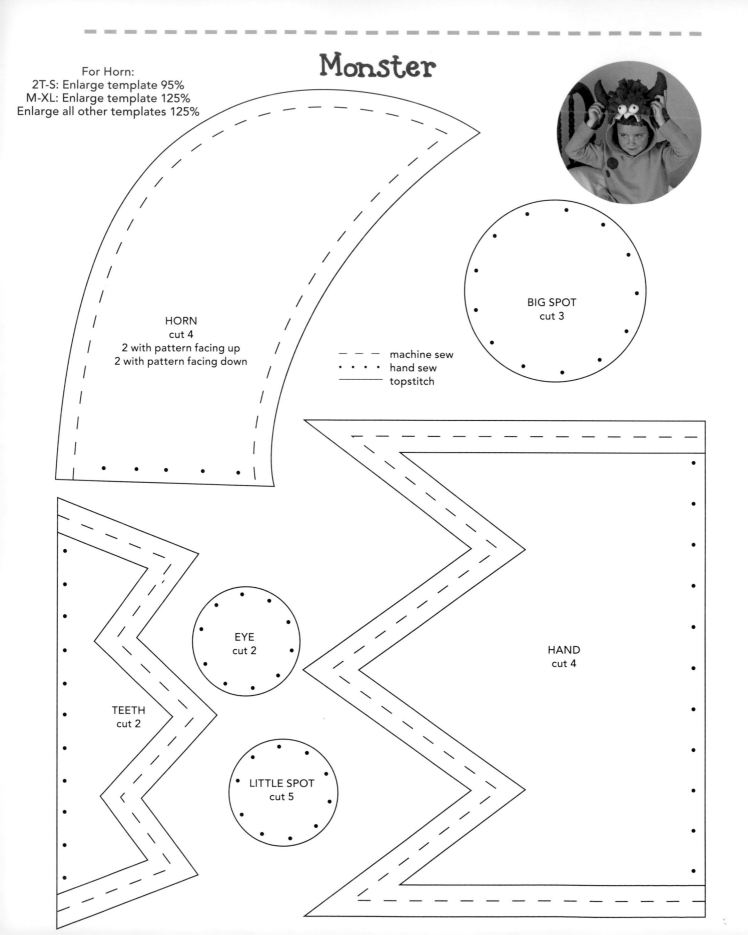

For Horn:
2T-S: Enlarge template 95%
M-XL: Enlarge template 125%
Enlarge all other templates 125%

HORN
cut 4
2 with pattern facing up
2 with pattern facing down

- - - - machine sew
· · · · hand sew
—— topstitch

BIG SPOT
cut 3

EYE
cut 2

TEETH
cut 2

LITTLE SPOT
cut 5

HAND
cut 4

Owl

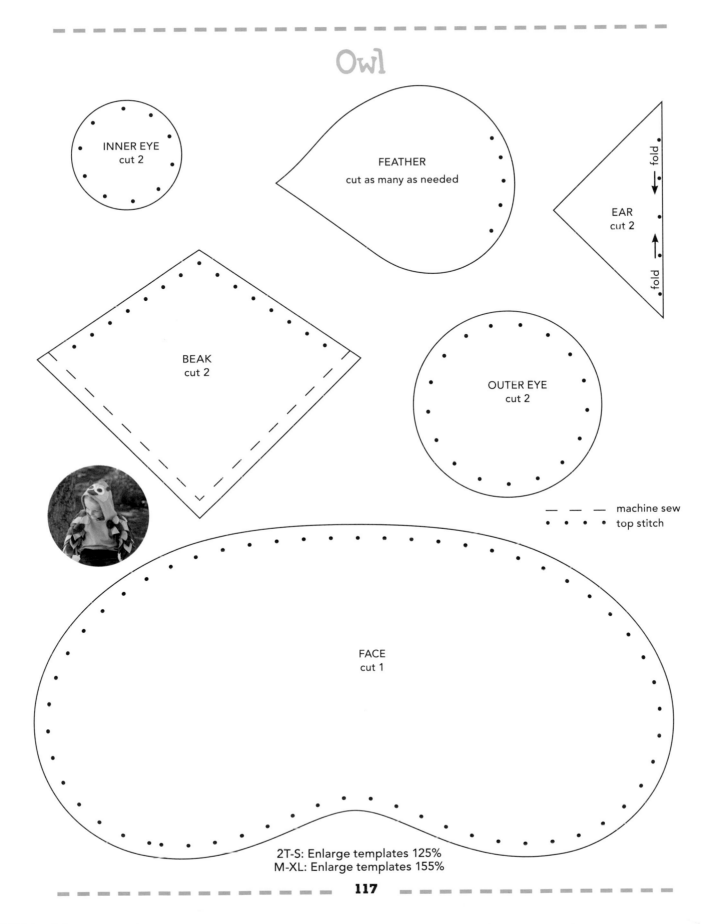

INNER EYE
cut 2

FEATHER
cut as many as needed

EAR
cut 2

fold

fold

BEAK
cut 2

OUTER EYE
cut 2

– – – machine sew
• • • top stitch

FACE
cut 1

2T-S: Enlarge templates 125%
M-XL: Enlarge templates 155%

Prince

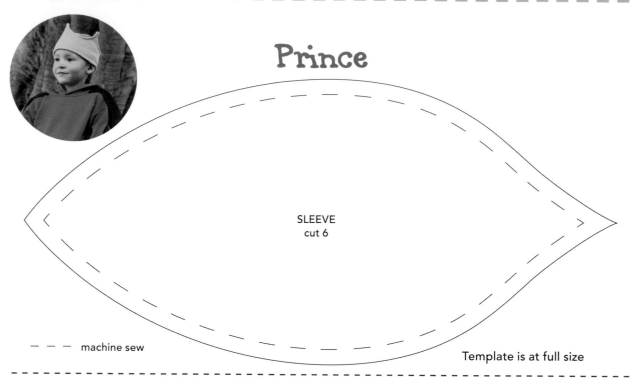

SLEEVE
cut 6

- - - - machine sew

Template is at full size

Puppy

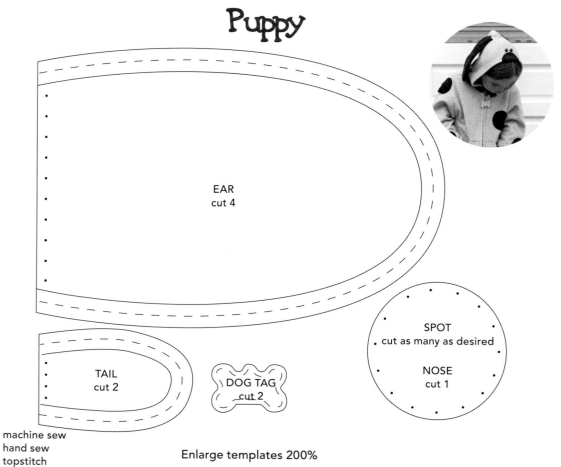

EAR
cut 4

TAIL
cut 2

DOG TAG
cut 2

SPOT
cut as many as desired

NOSE
cut 1

- - - - machine sew
· · · · hand sew
——— topstitch

Enlarge templates 200%

Rabbit

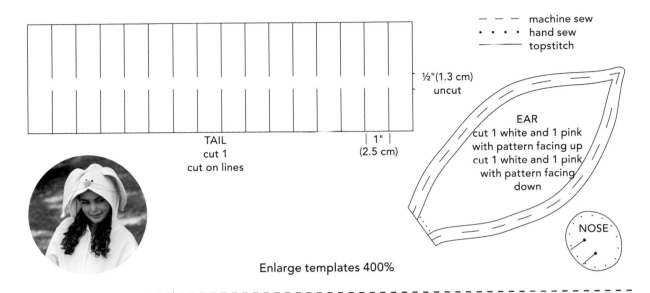

TAIL
cut 1
cut on lines

½"(1.3 cm)
uncut

| 1" |
(2.5 cm)

- – – machine sew
· · · · hand sew
——— topstitch

EAR
cut 1 white and 1 pink
with pattern facing up
cut 1 white and 1 pink
with pattern facing
down

NOSE

Enlarge templates 400%

Shark

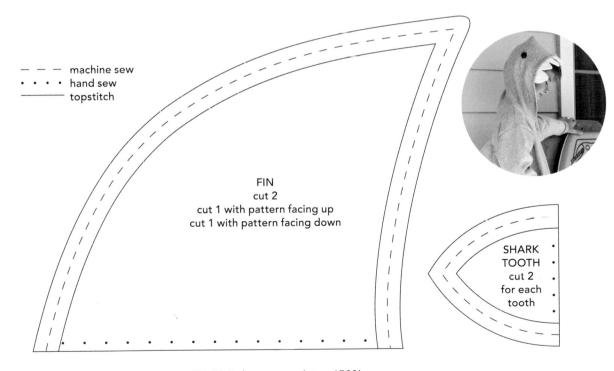

- – – machine sew
· · · · hand sew
——— topstitch

FIN
cut 2
cut 1 with pattern facing up
cut 1 with pattern facing down

SHARK
TOOTH
cut 2
for each
tooth

2T-4T: Enlarge templates 150%
S-XL: Enlarge templates 200%

Superhero

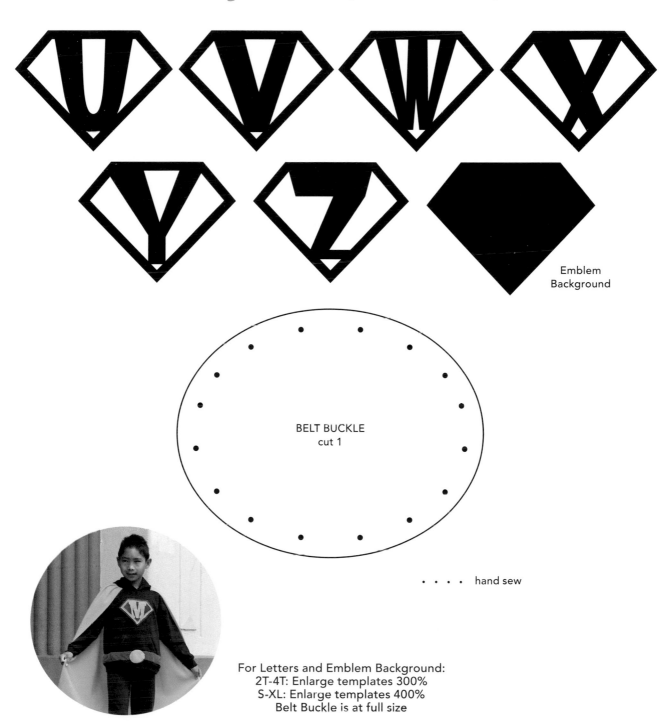

Emblem
Background

BELT BUCKLE
cut 1

• • • • hand sew

For Letters and Emblem Background:
2T-4T: Enlarge templates 300%
S-XL: Enlarge templates 400%
Belt Buckle is at full size

Unicorn

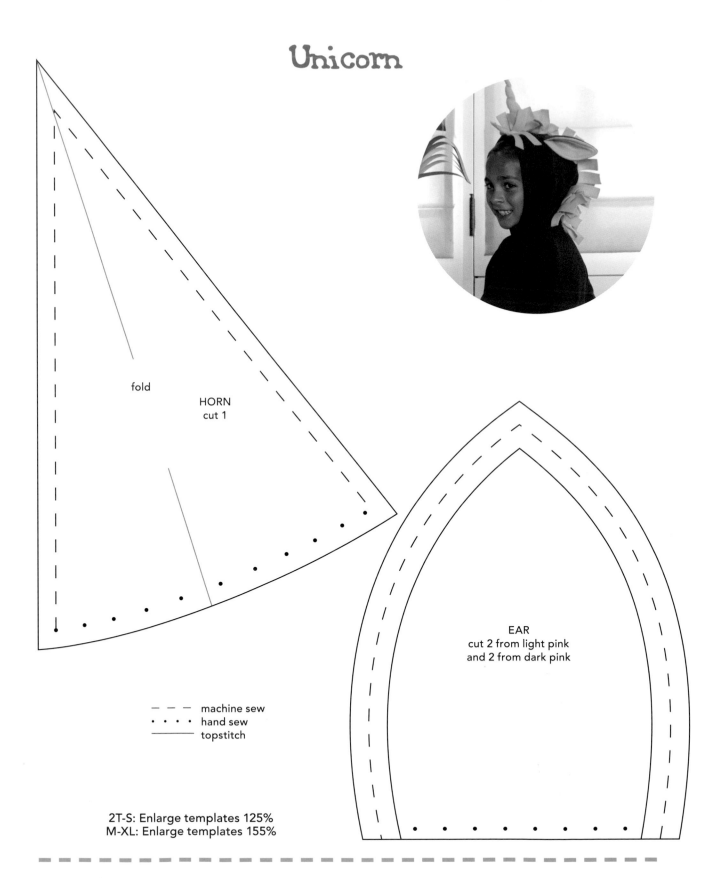

fold

HORN
cut 1

EAR
cut 2 from light pink
and 2 from dark pink

— — — machine sew
• • • • hand sew
——— topstitch

2T-S: Enlarge templates 125%
M-XL: Enlarge templates 155%

Wizard

. . . . hand sew

MOON
cut 3

STAR
cut 5 for cape
cut 3 for hat

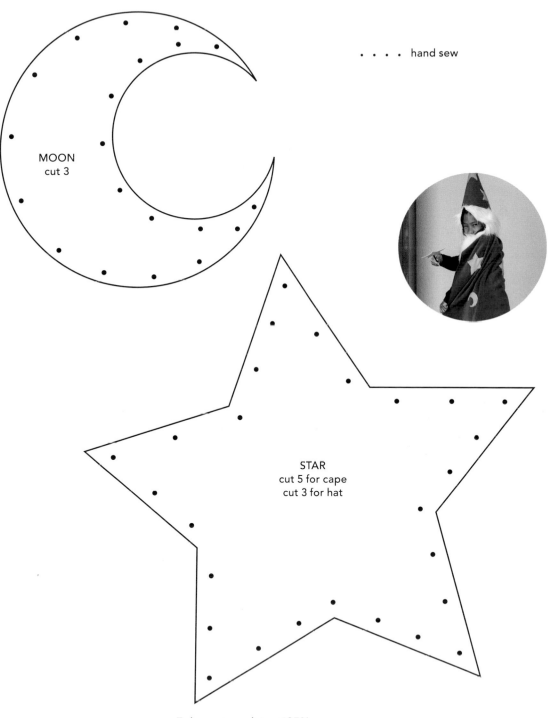

Enlarge templates 125%

Outtakes

Seriously. That's the first and last time I eat brussel sprouts.

You look bee-autiful dahling!

What? Do I have something on my face?

I'm ready for my close-up!

About the author

Mary Rasch resides in northern Minnesota near the shore of Lake Superior. She is always passionate about the creative process, whether she is sewing, knitting, painting, drawing, or shooting photos. Mary frequently teaches classes, writes about her family crafting projects in *Moms and Dads Today*, and photographs local families (see maryrasch.com for recent happenings). She is the author of *Fleece Hat Friends* (Lark Crafts, 2012), and her work has been featured in publications such as *Stash Happy: Felt* (Lark Crafts, 2011). Mary is equally passionate about her family—she is married to a very supportive, fun-loving man, and has a beautiful son and daughter who bless her life with humor, chaos, love, and fulfillment.

Acknowledgments

How can I begin to say thank you to those who are closest to me? To my husband, Troy, the first one I bounced ideas off of, I appreciate your support and constant encouragement ... and thanks for giving me that sewing machine on our first Christmas together. Thank you to Michael and Natalie, my little ones, for your patience as I worked on this project. Thanks for trying on costume after costume and going to the fabric store almost every day. I am grateful to my parents and in-laws who whisked away our kiddos for weekends of fun so I could double-time my work.

It was an absolute joy to work with Shannon Quinn-Tucker (Editor) as she made this dream a reality. Thanks also go to Amanda Carestio for her editorial oversight. I appreciate all who gave their talents to produce Playful Hoodies, including Carol Barnao (Art Director), Cynthia Shaffer (Photographer), Orrin Lundgren (Template Illustrations), Kathy Brock (Technical Editor), and Karen Levy (Proofreader).

Index

Credits

Editors: Shannon Quinn-Tucker and Amanda Carestio

Art Director: Carol Barnao

Illustrator: Mary Rasch

Templates: Orrin Lundgren

Photographer: Cynthia Shaffer

Cover Designer: Carol Barnao

Special thanks to Alexis Marie Allen, Audrina Victoria Allen, Kolbey Cirks, Abby Costello, Calem Costello, Miles Costello, Tiffany Jo Curtis, Jacob Eusebio, Ella Furry, Cael Hensley, Alivia Pacino, Luke Schlesinger, Jessica Spotts, Flynn Staab, Marisol Staab, and Declan Sullivan, who served as models.